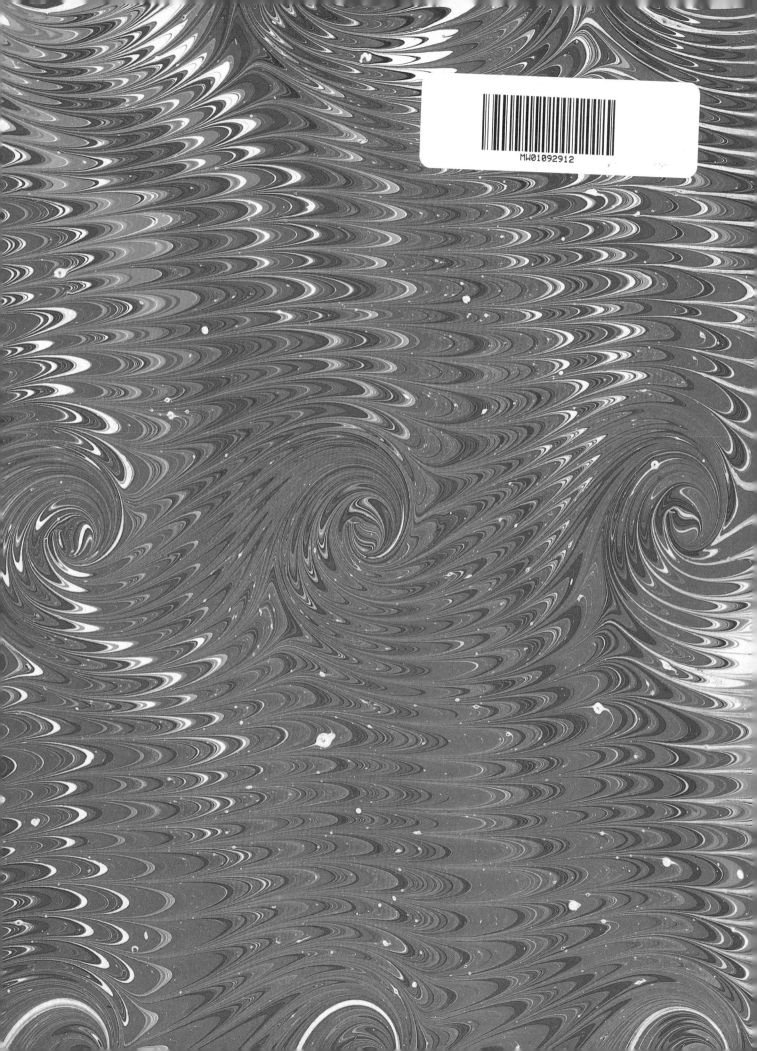

Reflections on
American
Brilliant Cut Glass

Bill & Louise Boggess

With
Value
Guide

77 Lower Valley Road, Atglen, PA 19310

Dedication

Dedicated to the members of the American Cut Glass Association

ALSO BY LOUISE BOGGESS:

Fiction Techniques That Sell
Writing Articles That Sell
Writing Fillers That Sell
Journey To Citizenship
Your Social Security Benefits
Article Techniques That Sell
Writing Fiction That Sells
How To Write Fillers and Short Features That Sell
How To Write Short Stories That Sell

Audio Cassettes:

How To Write Short Stories That Sell
Article Techniques That Sell

Video Cassettes:

How To Write Short Stories That Sell
Article Techniques That Sell

With Husband Bill:

American Brilliant Cut Glass
Identifying American Brilliant Cut Glass
Identifying American Brilliant Cut Glass, Revised and Enlarged Edition
Collecting American Brilliant Cut Glass

COVER

Overlay ruby-cut-to-clear punch bowl in the Star Pattern made at John O'Conner's American Cut Glass Company, given as a gift to his daughter, Mary

Published by Schiffer Publishing, Ltd.
77 Lower Valley Road
Atglen, PA 19310
Please write for a free catalog.
This book may be purchased from the publisher.
Please include $2.95 postage.
Try your bookstore first.

We are interested in hearing from authors
with book ideas on related subjects.

Key for Price Guide

S=Standard cut
C=Choice, has extra features
P=Premium
L=Limited

To simplify and make the Value Guide more usable, we have divided all of the illustrations into four categories: Standard, Choice, Premium, and Limited.

A STANDARD piece consists of a clear blank, fairly simple pattern, and a common shape.

A CHOICE piece adds these features to the standard characteristics: a more ornate pattern, larger or smaller size, variance in shape, and a quality addition of a stopper lid, handles, or a foot.

A PREMIUM piece retains the best features of a Standard and Choice one and combines them with sharpness in cutting, very ornate or highly simplified pattern, excellent polish, unique shape, and at least one or more quality extras.

LIMITED describes museum-type pieces or colored glass that defy evaluation but depend on what the buyer will pay.

Before each caption number of an illustration, we have placed the key letter of th ssification: S, C, P, and L. To effectively use the Value Guide, find an illustration comparable to your piece in shape and pattern. It need not exactly duplicate your piece. Find the shape and the letter in the Value Guide to learn the price range.

Copyright © 1995 by Bill and Louise Boggess

Printed in the United States of America.
ISBN: 0-88740-722-6

Library of Congress Cataloging-in-Publication Data

Boggess, Bill.
    Reflections on American brilliant cut glass: with value guide/Bill & Louise Boggess.
        p.   cm.
    Includes bibliographical references (p. -) and indexes.
    ISBN 0-88740-722-6 (hard)
    1. Cut glass—United States—History—19th century. 2. Cut glass—United States—History—20th century. I. Boggess, Louise.
II. Title.
NK5203.B65   1995
748.2913'09'034075--dc20
                                       95-5450
                                       CIP

Contents

Acknowledgements

We sincerely value the assistance of those who share our appreciation of American brilliant cut glass. The following members of the American Cut Glass Association contributed both photographs and information:

Gerald Ampe, Dowlton and Ruth Anne Berry, Lloyd and Barbara Bishop, Dr. Kenneth Braunstein, Maurice Crofford, Marty Cohen, Tom DeGraffenried, B. Dinelli, George Dunford, Bill and Jeanne Evans, Donald Griesbach, Dave and Chris Janke, Donnie and Suzzy Kosterman, Steven and Joyce Kuhns, Michael La Bate, Carrol Lyle, Dean and Jackie Marsh, Stephen Mey, Roberta Mocabee, Paul Miles, Jack Neberall, Denny and Cheri Parks, Al and Barbara Pierce, E. M. Ramey, Tom Roth, Stephen Schwartz, Robert and Valerie Smith, Stephen Smith, Sam and Becky Story, Eddie and Joan Sullivan, Bob Tobey, Don Tooze, Leon and Carol Torline, John and Joan Watterson, Bob and Jan Wiersma, Curtis Whiticar, Phil and Kathy Yonge, and Rev. Ellsworth Young.

Dowlton and Ruth Anne Berry provided the most black and white and colored photos including that for the cover of the book. Tom and Vickie Matthews furnished photographs of the cutting process. Rene Lawrie of Lightner Museum sent photographs of the steps in cutting and the present pattern used in the White House. Ed McCartney sketched the table for photographing cut glass.

Appreciation goes to these who shared their extensive file of photographs: Jacquelyn Fishel, Bob Hall (A Touch of Glass Ltd.), Dick and Joan Randles (The Cutter's Wheel), and Tom and Vickie Matthews (Glass Studios Ltd.).

Walter Poeth assisted with identification of patterns and the value guide. Sam and Becky Story expanded our information on H. P. Sinclaire and Val St. Lambert.

Frances L. Graham (ANTIQUES & COLLECTING HOBBIES), Kyle D. Husfloen (THE ANTIQUE TRADER WEEKLY), Linda Kruger (COLLECTORS NEWS & THE ANTIQUE REPORTER), and Tom O'Connor (GLASS COLLECTOR'S DIGEST) published our articles on American brilliant cut glass. We expanded these articles into chapters for this book.

We sincerely appreciate Peter B. Schiffer, our publisher, whose encouragement inspired us to write this book, and Jeffrey B. Snyder, our editor.

Finally, we thank many others who bought our previous books and continually asked us about the next one.

Bill and Louise Bogges

Preface

Knowledge increases the pleasure of collecting brilliant cut glass. Whether a collector or a dealer, the more you know, the more you want to know. This book endeavors to expand old information and to introduce new, carefully researched facts.

We have researched this information from three different sources. Much information came from these printed sources: approximately 135 old catalogs, patent records, and magazine advertisements of the era. To these facts we have added interviews with people who worked in the glass industry and descendants of company owners. Finally collectors and dealers have shared much information, helping us to identify an unknown because it duplicated a signed piece. We have tried to relate the facts from all of these sources and have drawn a few indicated deductions.

By eliminating boring repetition, we have presented certain facts in a simple format. Many of you wanted sizes of pieces. Whenever possible we have provided measurements. Since cut glass measures in inches, we give the number and indicate the diameter with a "D" and the height with an "H" which eliminates the repeating of "inches." For pieces, such as celeries or trays, we give two dimensions, but some shapes required three measurements. In referring to factories or cutting shops we state the full company name when first mentioned. After that we use the name of the man who headed the company, such as Libbey or Hawkes, or shorten the name of a firm, such as Empire or Sandwich.

In regard to the names of shapes and function, we have used those common to a majority of major companies, such as "jug" for "pitcher" or "comport" for "compote." Of course, you can always find specific exceptions in any case.

We have tried to eliminate duplication in identifications given in our other two books. We did repeat a very few patterns with unusual shapes to show a uniqueness or to fulfil a special purpose as stated in the accompanying information.

We have earnestly tried to accurately match photographs of cut glass in every detail to a catalog illustration. If we made any errors, and we could very easily, please let us know so we can make corrections.

We sincerely wish that the information in this book expands your present knowledge and makes collecting or buying American brilliant cut glass more exciting.

Bill and Louise Boggess

What is beautiful is a joy for all seasons. — Oscar Wilde

CHAPTER 1 *An Era Of Brilliance*

The Centennial Exposition that opened on July 4, 1876, in Philadelphia, introduced the Brilliant Period of American cut glass. For the next forty years the Americans transformed small glass companies into an artistic industry that dominated the production of brilliant cut glass (P 1). To accomplish this feat, American companies took advantage of every opportunity.

NATURAL RESOURCES

The United States contained an abundance of ingredients necessary for the production of glass. The plentiful resources played a major role in this leadership.

1. Sand (Silica)

The Americans found white sand or almost pure silica plentiful along the coastal and river areas. Silica provides the main ingredient for glass making. A number of glass factories and cutting shops clustered around these sandy areas. A factory did the total job: made the metal, blew the blanks, designed and cut the patterns. The cutting shop bought the blanks from the factory, then designed and cut the pattern.

2. Water

Areas abundant with sand generally contained a large supply of nearby water. Water provided the source for electricity which powered the cutting wheels (2). Electricity resulted in an even control of the wheels when cutting the blank.

P 1. A tray (10 x 16) in a brilliant pattern.

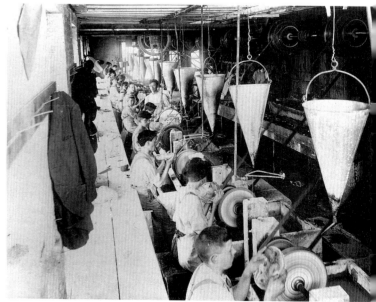

2. Cutting shop of F. X. Parsche and Son Company.

3. Gas and Petroleum

Gas supplied an even heat under the closed, cylindrical vessels or monkey pots that held the mixture for making the molten metal. The controlled temperature evenly fused the ingredients and resulted in a clearer metal from which to blow glass. In the Brilliant Period the Americans replaced gas with petroleum, equally good and in abundance.

4. Lead

Another necessity for making glass included lead, also found in abundance. The Americans removed the impurities from the molten metal with lead oxide. The amount of lead oxide added to the metal depended on the individual company. Some added as much as 60%. Supposedly, H. C. Fry added the most lead to blanks, but he never revealed his formula.

William Gillinder in his book of glass formulas recommended this formula as one of the best for cut glass.

Sand............... 336 lbs.
Lead............... 224 lbs.
Ash................. 112 lbs.
Mitre.............. 28 lbs.
Arsenic............ 1 oz.
Manganese..... 2 oz.

Do note the large amount of lead.

Lead oxide not only added weight to the blank but also provided, according to an old cutter, the "softness" needed for easy cutting. Other characteristics of lead included prismatic clarity when polished and a resonant ring when thumped.

IMPROVE PROCEDURES

The more ornate patterns and the increase in production demanded more systematic procedures in cutting glass.

1. Curved Miter

Cutting wheels varied in thickness, diameter, and shape of the edge (3). For example, a wheel with a rounded edge produced a hollow cut, a flat edge did a panel, and a v-shaped edge made a miter. The cutter needed a large number of wheels, ranging from very small to large. By the 1880s, the master craftsman began to design ornate patterns with curved miters.

Americans soon learned to turn the piece when cutting with a v-shaped or sharp edge wheel to provide a curved miter. The length of the curved miter depended on the size of the wheel. A short curve needed only a small wheel, but a 6-inch curve required a much larger wheel.

3. Two different angle miter wheels and a punt wheel on fast change shaft ends.

2. Assembly Line

Perhaps the greatest change in procedures consisted of assembly-line production (4). The master craftsman designed the pattern. The rougher worked from a model or a pattern sketch. For more accuracy in cutting occasionally the craftsman drew the miter outline on the blank with a wax pencil.

When the rougher finished the pattern outline, the smoother added the major and minor motifs. Then the polisher removed the whiteness caused by cutting with a wooden wheel and pumice. Next he polished with brushes and finally finished with felt (5). So each craftsman became an expert in the cutting routine. This specialization provided superior cut glass by trained experts.

3. Acid Polish

When hand buffing did not remove the whiteness from ornate patterns, companies introduced acid polish. An acid bath offered a cheaper, quicker, and easier method of polishing. When the smoother finished, the polisher placed the article in a wire basket and lowered it into a tank containing an acid mixture. The polisher wore protective clothing and a mask (6). A fan above the tank blew away the fumes. A perfect polishing depended on the strength of the acid and exact timing. If left too long in the acid, a raininess appeared on the uncut spaces and the deep miters. Hand polishing could remove this raininess. Some companies generally did some hand polishing while others did not.

MANPOWER

The availability of foreign manpower contributed considerably to the leadership of American companies. Since European countries seemed to face one depression after another, these foreign workers considered the United States a land of plenty. In turn, the American companies welcomed these experienced craftsmen, especially those in management.

4. Steps in cutting glass. Courtesy of Lightner Museum.

5. First step in hand polishing, using a treated fiber wheel and pumice.

6. Acid polishing a piece of cut glass.

1. Management

Many of these emigrants grew up in glass making. Often they represented several generations of glass makers. As an example, John Hoare, born in Cork, Ireland, apprenticed at companies located in Belfast and Birmingham. He then worked for Thomas Webb and Sons in England before coming to the United States in 1853.

In 1867, Hoare persuaded T. G. Hawkes to join him in the United States. Hawkes, born in Surmont, Ireland, descended from two families well-known in glass making: the Penroses of Waterford and the Dudleys of England. When Hawkes organized his own company in the United States, he employed Oliver Egginton, Henry P. Sinclaire, Jr., and Thomas Hunt, to name a few. Later each of these men established their own company.

Christian Dorflinger came from the St. Louis Works in St. Louis, France. He influenced F. X. Parsche (7) to come to the United States from Meriden, Bohemia. L. Straus came from Bavaria. Companies in the United States also provided leaders, such as W. L. Libbey, H. C. Fry, T. B. Clark, and Charles Tuthill.

7. Another view of the F. X. Parsche cutting shop.

2. Skilled Craftsmen

Glass companies needed skilled and innovative craftsmen to create new patterns and motifs. Traditional procedures in Europe limited the ingenuity of these skilled craftsmen. In the United States with few if any traditions, the workers could express their creativity. So they welcomed the opportunity to come to the United States.

Occasionally, heads of companies went to Europe to entice artisans to come to the United States. Generally speaking, they needed little encouragement. Mount Washington Glass Works hired such skilled artisans as Andrew Snow, Jr., Thomas Singleton, Jr., and Albert Steffins. So the Americans worked alongside of the foreign craftsmen to master glass production.

American craftsmen included Phillip McDonald who created the Russian pattern for Hawkes. William R. Eliot worked for Meriden Cut Glass Company, Benjamin Davies cut for L. Straus and Sons, John S. O'Connor for Dorflinger. Libbey relied on Solon O. Richardson, D. F. Spillane, William Marrett, George Hatch, and especially William C. Anderson.

Glass companies needed other types of craftsmen, too. Some took care of mixing the metal. Others formed a shop for making the blank. A shop consisted of a gatherer, blower, a servitor to reheat the glass, and a gaffer to apply a foot or handles. So the American companies welcomed these employees but at the same time developed workmen from their own localities.

3. Apprentices

The American companies looked to the future and began to train apprentices for glass production. Some apprentices started work as early as age 13. They trained through the different stages of glass production. J. D. Bergen apprenticed at the Co-Operative Cut Glass Company in Brooklyn, New York. A son or relative of a company owner would work as an apprentice to learn more about glass production. When he completed an apprenticeship, normally he received a management job in the family company.

ACHIEVING RECOGNITION

No matter how excellent the product, it needed extensive recognition to attract buyers. American companies decided to acquaint the world with brilliant cut glass.

1. Expositions

Expositions offered contact with large groups of buyers. In 1889, Hawkes received outstanding recognition at the Paris Exposition for American cut glass (8). An American exposition normally celebrated an historical event. In 1903, at the Lewis and Clark Exposition President William McKinley defined "exposition" as the time-keeper of progress. Companies tried to show progress with displays of outstanding pieces of cut glass. Usually one company provided the focal point with a rare piece of brilliant cut glass created especially for the exposition. Most of the glass exhibitors sold souvenirs (9) for the visitors to take home. The exhibition caught the attention of royalty and heads of governments, and they purchased state dinner sets.

8. Certificate awarded to T. G. Hawkes at the Paris Exposition, 1889.

C 9. A souvenir hatchet (7.5) sold by Libbey at 1893 Exposition in Chicago.

2. Home Markets

Near the turn of the century a new, wealthy class developed from the growth of heavy industry in the United States. These families--Duponts, Rockefellers, Vanderbilts, Astors, to name a few--bought large dinner sets for lavish entertainment. They elaborately decorated their homes with vases (P 10), covered comports (C 11) or lamps (C 12).

Companies readily recognized a growing middle class that bought cut glass piece-by-piece. For them a piece of brilliant cut glass became their first choice as a gift for a wedding, anniversary, birthday, or retirement. An engraving on pieces with silver tops gave initials (C 13), name and date (C 14), or information on the presentation (P 15). The engraving on this tobacco jar stated: "Presented to Theodore Brunwald by members of his office force Christmas 1896."

Companies made the glass easily available in jewelry or department stores. Some companies listed the glass in mail order catalogs, such as Marshall Field or Sears-Roebuck. Advertising constantly expanded in other directions. In women's magazines the advertisements pictured pieces of glass with the name of the company so the buyer could ask for a special shape or design. Some magazines rewarded a new or renewed subscription with a small item of cut glass. Many other groups selected cut glass as prizes for contests. At home and abroad, consumers soon recognized American brilliant cut glass as the finest in the world. So if someone challenges your statement, quote these facts and turn doubters into believers.

P 10. An ornate vase (8.5 D x 14 H) cut in rows.

C 11. Covered comport (9.5 D x 7.5 H).

C 12. A typical cut glass lamp (13 H).

C 14. The engraved lid on this puff box (6.5 D x 4.5 H) contains a name
and date.

C 13. The sterling lid on this jar (3.5 D x 5.5 H) has engraved initials.

P 15. A tobacco jar (7 D x 6 H) has a total presentation inscription.

CHAPTER 2 *Cutting The Blank*

When you mention brilliant cut glass, some people immediately visualize a heavy blank with an elaborate, geometric pattern. A blank refers to the uncut shape. Geometric describes only one style of cutting (P 16). Increased competition between companies led to different styles of cutting.

A quick check of company catalogs, patent records, or advertisements in old magazines show the different styles used to decorate blanks during the Brilliant Period. These pattern overlapped in time during the forty years of the Brilliant Period, but the geometric patterns dominated. In fact, some companies produced only geometric designs throughout the Brilliant Period, but others introduced different styles.

GEOMETRIC PATTERNS

A pattern consisted of a combination of a deep miter outline elaborated with major and minor motifs. Geometric motifs included such figures as parallel lines, squares, triangles, or circles found in geometry. The type of miter outline and the number of major and minor motifs made the difference between simple or ornate patterns.

1. Simple Patterns

Simple patterns consisted of an uncomplicated miter outline for the pattern with fewer and simpler motifs.

Outline. Bars formed a simple outline for the miters (S 17). In some patterns the bars intersected at the center and in others they formed an outer border near the edge of a piece to frame the motifs.

Another miter outline cut repetitive motifs in rows (S 18). The Strawberry-Diamond (S 19) and the Russian (C 20) patterns used this outline. The choice of motifs, the shape and size of the blank determined the number of rows.

A very popular outline included parallel miters with a border of geometric motifs (S 21). The decoration cut on the miters and the types of motifs in the border whether at top, at bottom, or both could simplify or elaborate the pattern (C 22).

S 17. A tray (13 D) cut in bars outline.

P 16. A handled, footed bowl (12 D x 6 H) in geometric brilliant cut.

S 18. A bowl (8 D) cut in rows outline.

S 21. A bowl (9 D x 4 H) in border and miter outline.

S 19. A leaf-shaped bonbon (4 x 6) in row outline of Strawberry-Diamond and Fan Pattern.

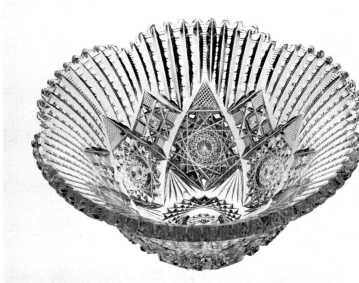

C 22. Bowl (9.5 D x 4 H) in border and miter outline.

C 20. A plate (6.25 D) in Russian, a rows outline.

Some companies outlined a star as the focal point (C 23). Different motifs filled the uncut spaces around the star in the center. Libbey and other companies cut a five-point star with combinations motifs to join the major ones (S 24).

A dual motif outline joined two dominant figures (C 25). A variant of this miter outline designed a combination of minor motifs to link the dominant ones together (C 26).

Motif. A simple pattern usually consisted of a major and two or three minor motifs. Simple major motifs included an 8-point star (C 27) or a hobstar with twelve to sixteen points (C 28). To add variety, the craftsman elongated either of the above motifs (C 29). A rayed or single star formed a major motif, but in most cases it decorated the underfoot of a comport (S 30), jug, or vase. Other major motifs filled a diamond shape with crosscut diamonds (C 31) or a triangle with crosshatching or cane (S 32).

Minor motifs endeavored to accent the major ones. Fans dominated as minor motifs, ranging from three to five prongs, always an odd number. Individual triangles or diamond shapes framed minor motifs of cane, nailhead diamonds, or crosshatching.

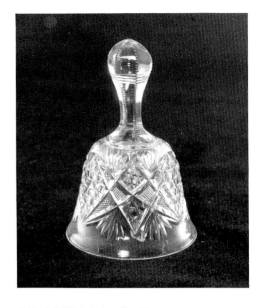

C 26. A bell (5 H) in dual motifs outline.

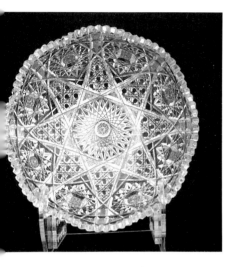

C 23. Bowl (8 D x 4 H) in star outline.

S 24. Handled nappy (7 D) motifs joined by stars.

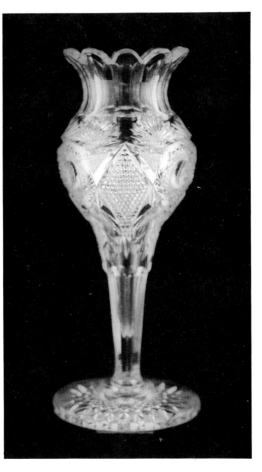

C 25. Vase (10 H) in dual motifs outline.

C 27. A vase (10 H) with an 8-point star as major motif.

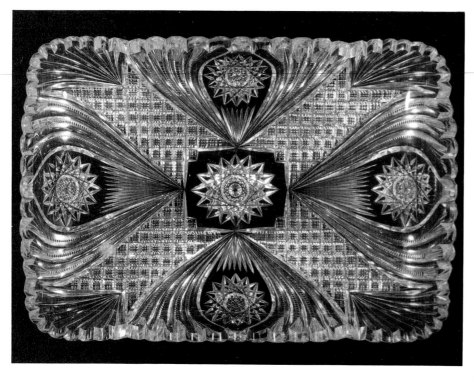

C 28. A tray (8 D x 12 H) with a hobstar as dominant motif.

S 30. A comport (6 x 6) with a rayed star on underfoot.

S 29. A handled, footed nappy (9 x 6 D) with major motif an elongated star.

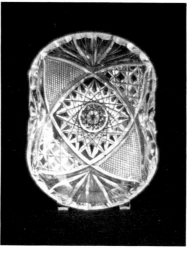

C 31. Grapefruit (5 D x 7.5) with dominant motif in crosscut diamonds and signed Clark.

S 32. Pin tray (4 x 3) with triangles of crosshatching and cane as dominant motifs.

2. Ornate Patterns

An ornate pattern included a more complicated miter outline and an increase in both old and new dominant motifs. By the 1890s, Libbey's patterns began to cover most of the blank. This competition pushed other companies to follow suit. Companies first tried to complicate the simple miter outlines, but new ones offered more opportunity for embellishment.

Outlines. To complicate the bars outline, companies adorned the bars with both major and minor motifs (C 33). Motifs in the rows outline grew more ornate (P 34). Ornate double borders decorated the border and miter outline (P 35).

A gothic or pointed arch (C 36) provided the basis for an elaborate pattern. The craftsman may close or leave the bottom of the arch open.

P 35. A comport (10.5 D x 14.5 H) with two borders in this border and miter outline.

C 33. A tray (8 x 17) with both major and minor motifs on the bars.

P 34. Bowl (8 D by 3.5 H) with more ornate major motifs of hobstars.

C 36. Bowl (8 D x 4 H) that follows a gothic arch outline for a more elaborate pattern.

A panels outline consisted of vertical divisions (C 37). The complexity of the design relied on the motifs that decorated the panels (C 38) and the number of different panels, usually more than one.

Halley's Comet inspired the swirls outline (C 39). The number and different types of swirls along with the decorating motifs complicated the outline.

Pointed Loops (C 40) formed an outline for a variety of ornate patterns. The ornateness depended upon the number of loops and the choice of motifs.

C 37. A nut dish (3 D x 2 H) with panels outline.

C 39. A plate (10 D) in swirls outline.

C 38. A vase (6 D x 14 H) in an ornate panels outline.

C 40. A bowl (10 D x 5 H) uses the pointed loops outline.

A circles outline (P 41) encouraged the use of curved miters.

The dual motifs outline covered almost every space on the blank (S 42). The combination of miter outlines (P 43) increased the complexity of the pattern.

Motifs. The Americans quickly recognized the need for more elaborate major motifs in the outlines. The craftsman cut the hobstar (S 44) with points that ranged in number to sixty-four around a raised center. The pinwheel (S 45) also whirled around a raised center. A clear center circled by notched miters characterized a sunburst motif (C 46). Fans between the prongs of a single star became a shooting one (C 47). A flashed star (S 48) added fans between the points of a hobstar. Some patterns blazed the points of a hobstar (C 49). The major motifs easily made a pattern more decorative.

P 41. A bowl (10 D x 5 H) relies on curves to make circles outline.

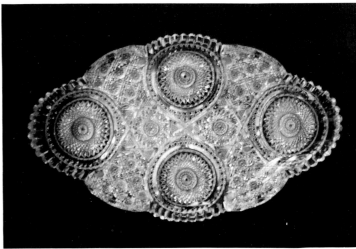

P 43. A tray (10.5 D x 17.5 D) that combines bars and circles outline for a more complicated pattern.

S 42. A comport (6 D by 6 H) where dual motifs cover the blank.

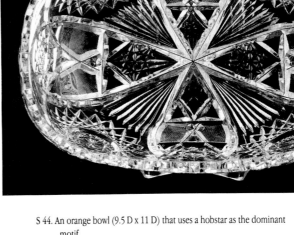

S 44. An orange bowl (9.5 D x 11 D) that uses a hobstar as the dominant motif.

C 47. A punch bowl (8 D x 8 H) focuses on a shooting star for a dominant motif.

S 45. A bowl (9 D x 3 H) with a pinwheel for a dominant motif.

S 48. Bowl (8 D x 3.5 H) cut with a flashed star.

C 46. A bowl (8.5 D x 3.5 H) has a dominant motif of a sunburst.

C 49. Fruit bowl (13.5 D x 6.5 H) with a blazed star.

In the minor motifs prongs of fans increased from five to eleven. Some companies cut fans between the prongs (C 50). Notching the prongs made them more decorative. Notching panels and flutes (S 51) made them more ornate. A combination of motifs filled pointed loops that linked the major ones (C 52).

The introduction of these new miter outlines and motifs enabled companies to greatly Americanize and complicate patterns. When interest seemed to wane in cut glass, companies chose other styles for cutting the blank.

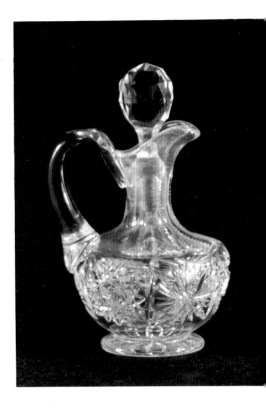

S 51. Oil (6 H) with notched flutes on neck.

C 50. Bowl (8 D x 3.5 H) with fans cut between fans.

C 52. Matching comports (10 D x 10 H) with a combination motifs filled the pointed loops.

C 53. A jug (8 H) in which Tuthill combines geometrics and intaglio poppy.

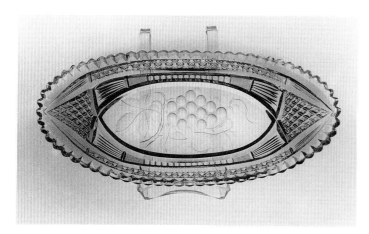

C 54. A fruit bowl (7 D x 13 H) that combines a geometric border with fruit in Grapes Pattern.

INTAGLIO OR STONE WHEEL ENGRAVING

Intaglio refers to engraving done with a stone wheel, the opposite of cameo. The artisan cut the pattern by looking through the blank when pressed against the stone wheel. At first the pattern maker frequently combined intaglio with geometric cutting.

1. Geometric and Intaglio

Soon after the turn of the century Charles Tuthill combined geometric borders with a variety of flowers or fruit. He left the intaglio engraving smokey but sharply polished the geometric motifs for good contrast (C 53). Fruit motifs with geometric borders consisted of mostly grapes (C 54). Another designer framed the intaglio flowers with a geometric border (C 55). On a unique jug panels of flowers alternated with ones of sharp diamonds (P 56).

C 55. A fruit bowl (6 D x 10 H) where a geometric border circles intaglio flower.

P 56. Jug (13 H) alternates panels of sharp diamonds with intaglio flowers.

2. Intaglio Only

Tuthill again took the lead and eliminated the geometric border. He emphasized a single type of flower, such as poppy (C 57), lily, or iris. Fruit motifs consisted of grapes, plums or combinations of two or more fruits.

As sales soared, Libbey, J. Hoare, and others began to cut intaglio only designs. Hawkes developed a special kind of intaglio he called "gravic glass" and signed it with a special signature (See appendix). Flowers completely covered a punch bowl (C 58) while another company decorated a jug with birds and flowers (C 59). From intaglio flowers and such, companies turned to copper wheel engraving.

COPPER WHEEL ENGRAVING

For copper wheel engraving the artisan worked with various sizes of small copper wheels fastened to a vertical stem. The engraver brought the blank up to the copper wheel, the opposite of geometric and intaglio, and cut from the top. This enabled him to see the design clearly and produce more detailed work. Copper wheel engraving required more training and an artistic talent for delicate designs.

1. Geometric and Engraving

H. P. Sinclaire favored copper wheel engraving as a delicate border of flowers for a geometric pattern. Possibly some of his most easily recognized combinations left a clear circle or medallion for engraved flowers (C 60). The medallions on some patterns contained the same flowers while other patterns used a variety of flowers. Sinclaire also used the geometric border to frame animals, birds, and scenes, to name a few (P 61). Other companies frequently intermingled floral engravings with geometric borders (C 62) or with a combination of bars and circles around the flowers (C 63).

C 57. A vase (6 D x 7 H) with intaglio Poppy only.

C 58. A punch bowl (14 D x 14 H) with intaglio flower entirely.

C 59. A jug (9.5 H) cut with bird and intaglio flower.

C 60. A tray (18 H) by Sinclaire in Diamond and Silver Threads where each medallion contains a different flower: Lilies of the Valley, Pansy, Rose, and Poppy.

P 61. A dish (4 D x 8 H) where geometric border surrounds a swan.

C 62. A bonbon (5.5 x 7.5 D) combines a geometric border with engraved flowers.

C 63. A bowl (8.5 D x 3.5 H) contains a bars and circles outline around the engraved flowers.

2. Engraving Only

As in intaglio patterns, engraving focused mostly on designs from nature. Flowers seemed most popular while fruit, scenes, and animals presented a challenge. As production costs soared, companies looked for cheaper methods of cutting glass with motifs from nature.

COST PRODUCTION PATTERNS

Near the end of the forty years, companies explored ways to reduce the cost of cutting glass. They put into operation the following procedures.

1. Craftsmen

A European war seemed on the horizon. Talented craftsmen who developed outstanding patterns decided to take jobs in other industries. Glass companies limited the creativity of new cutters and therefore paid them less. Some of the larger companies, such as Libbey, simplified previous patterns but kept the same name.

2. Figured or Molded Blanks

H. C. Fry Glass Company introduced the molded blank. Blowing the shape into a mold that contained most of the pattern reduced the cost of production. While the total designs included stems for the flower, the craftsman cut only the blossom (S 64). Any geometric cutting, such as divisions or a border, the mold contained (S 65). You can recognize the molded blank by the smoothness to the touch of the leaves or geometric cuts.

Acid polished the few cut parts. Some companies did recut the molded parts and then polished them. The second polishing removed any raininess. The recutting and double polish made the figured patterns more difficult to recognize.

Pieces blown into a mold show a slight grayish tint. Look for this slight discoloration. Sometimes you need to place the piece beside a finely cut, old one. The grayish tone resulted from less lead and more potash in the formula as well as the blowing in a mold.

S 65. A bowl (8 C x 3.5 H) with geometric bars between flowers on a figured blank.

REVIVAL PATTERNS

Again when interest lessened in cut glass, several large companies reactivated their finest geometric patterns (C 66) from previous years or cut completely new ones. Hawkes introduced the Panel Pattern and Meriden Cut Glass Company, the Alhambra. This revival movement, however, came too late to save the Brilliant Period.

World War I hastened the final end of the true Brilliant Period. Since lead went to war, the lack of it reduced the supply of good blanks. In addition, war restricted international and domestic sales.

After the war those companies that survived turned to decorating thin blanks with engraving or acid etching. Today American brilliant cut glass has becomes a highly desirable antique (C 67).

C 66. A jug (14 H) in geometric pattern from the Revival Period.

S 64. Bowl (8 D x 3.5 H) with only flowers cut on a figured blank.

C 67. Matching comports (7 D x 8 H) in American brilliant cut glass.

During the early years of the Brilliant Period, companies created a number of basic patterns that covered most of the blank. The two most popular, the Russian and the Strawberry-Diamond, continued in production throughout the forty years but with some modifications.

These changes in basic patterns resulted from the rising cost of production, growing competition between companies, and the need to attract new buyers. Often knowing the changes a particular company made can identify both the source and the pattern.

THE RUSSIAN PATTERN

The name Russian resulted from a series of incidents. In St. Petersburg around 1880, a United States ambassador bet a Russian nobleman that the Americans produced the finest cut glass in the world. To prove his statement, the ambassador ordered pieces of cut glass from Richard Briggs, an agent. On July 20, 1882, Phillip McDonald patented a heavily cut pattern for Hawkes. Briggs selected this pattern from Hawkes to send to Russia. When the pieces arrived, the nobleman took one look and, without hesitation, paid the bet.

In 1885, the Imperial Russian Embassy in Washington ordered a complete banquet service in this pattern. In that year, too, the American Embassy in St. Petersburg bought a state dinner service in this particular pattern. Because of these orders the pattern became known as "Russian" and appeared under this name in catalogs by Hawkes and other companies.

The pattern, as originally patented, consisted of alternating rows of pyramidal stars and hobnails decorated with a single or radial star. This particular pattern circled a hobstar of twenty-four points on the base of a plate, bowl or tray (C 68).

In 1886, the White House ordered a dinner service in Russian with an engraved seal of the United States. The use of this pattern continued until 1938, when President Franklin D. Roosevelt ordered a less expensive pattern in Renaissance (S 69) by Dorflinger.

1. Star Changes

In another replacement order of the Russian Pattern from the White House Dorflinger reduced the number of points in the center hobstar from twenty-four to twenty and narrowed the width of the border (C 70). In one Russian pattern Hawkes added a ring of enlarged points that framed the center hobstar (C 71). To cut production costs, Dorflinger substituted a single or radial star for the hobstar in the center of the base on a plate or bowl (C 72). To compete, Hawkes varied the length of alternate rays in the single star on the base center (C 73). By 1885, the New England Glass Company cut a raised star on the center of the base (C 74) and a hobstar on the hobnail. Dorflinger then enlarged the pyramidal star in the row and called the pattern Brilliante (C 75).

C 68. A plate (8 D) signed Hoare shows the original Russian Pattern.

S 69. President Franklin D. Roosevelt replaced the Russian Pattern with the Renaissance Pattern in the White House dinner service in 1938. A goblet shows the Renaissance Pattern. (Courtesy of Lightner Museum).

C 70. A plate (6 D) by Dorflinger who reduced the width of the border and the number of points in the center star.

C 71. A plate (7 D) in Russian Pattern Hawkes changed by adding a ring of points around the center star.

C 74. A bowl (9 D x 3.5 H) cut by New England Glass Company in 1885, used a raised star on the base.

C 72. A plate (7 D) in Russian by Dorflinger who changed the hobstar on the base to a radial one.

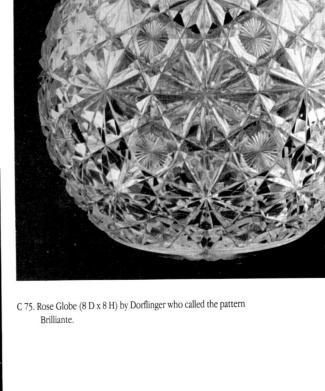

C 75. Rose Globe (8 D x 8 H) by Dorflinger who called the pattern Brilliante.

C 73. An ice cream plate (6 D) cut by Hawkes varied length of the rays in the single star.

Almost from the beginning Hawkes completely cut small pieces in Russian without a star on the base as in a sugar and cream (C 76). With a footed master salt, even the foot contained the Russian Pattern (C 77). The elimination of the center star on the base spread to larger shapes as in a bowl (C 78) and a hanging globe (P 79). In another change Hoare added a fan border and called the pattern Russian and Fan (C 80).

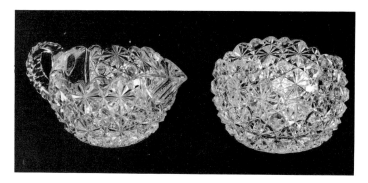

C 76. A small sugar and cream set Hawkes cut totally in the Russian Pattern.

C 77. A master salt (3.5 D x 2.5 H) cut entirely in the Russian Pattern.

C 78. A bowl (10 x 12.5) featured the original Russian Pattern.

C 79. A hanging globe (6 D x 6 H) contained no star on the base.

C 80. A claret in Russian and Fan by Hoare.

C 82. A covered cheese and plate (9 D x 7 H) supposedly ordered for the
White House by President Grover Cleveland has a clear hobnail.

2. Changes in the Hobnail

Changing the design on the hobnail occasionally resulted in a new pattern name. Both Hawkes and Hoare cut a hobstar on the hobnail and called the pattern Persian (C 81). When President Grover Cleveland ordered replacements, he reduced the cost by leaving the hobnail clear (C 82). While some refer to the clear hobnail pattern as Cleveland, to date no record verifies this fact. Another change in the hobnail included an 8-point star (C 83) on the hobnail of a carafe. Fry crosshatched the hobnail for a covered cheese and plate (S 84). The floral border on the underplate suggests a marriage, but both pieces contain the signature. A pattern on a butter tub alternated a flat star and crosshatching on the Russian Pattern around a pinwheel (C 85). One company cut a jug with only the pyramidal star and omitted the hobnail (S 86).

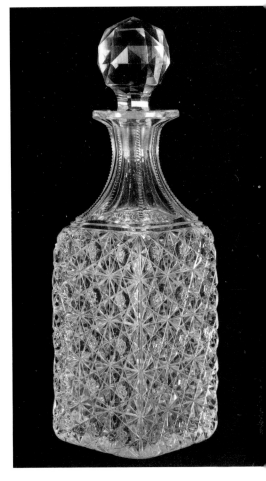

C 81 A square decanter (9.5 H) in Persian Pattern cut by
both Hawkes and Hoare.

S 83. A carafe (5.5 D x 7.5 H) has an 8-point star on the hobnail.

S 84. A covered cheese (12.5 D x 9.5 H) signed Fry has a crosshatched
hobnail. The floral underplate suggests a marriage.

C 85. An ice tub (6.5 D x 4 H) alternated a crosshatched hobnail with a flat star in the Russian Pattern that surrounded the pinwheel.

C 86. A jug (9 D x 6.5 H) omitted the hobnail and cut only the pyramidal star.

3. Pattern Alterations

Hawkes, Hoare, and Mount Washington divided the Russian Pattern with clear, wide miters (C 87) that made the original Russian design more dominant. Hoare cut the Wheat Pattern with alternating Russian and leafy sprigs (C 88) in swirls. In Russian and Pillars Hawkes swirled the pattern with alternating Russian and triple miters.

C 87. Three different companies divided a square bowl (10 D x 8 H) with clear miters at the corners.

C 88. A small cologne in Wheat Pattern by Hoare alternated a swirl of Russian with a leafy design.

C 89. A spoon and fork set signed Hawkes contains the Russian Pattern on the handles.

C 90. A paper weight (3.5 x 2) in Russian.

The Russian Pattern, or parts of it, decorated other shapes. Russian proved a favorite on handles of punch servers or for a salad fork and spoon set signed Hawkes (C 89). Whimsies and small pieces, such as a paper weight (C 90), favored the Russian Pattern. The Russian Pattern shared equally with hobstars on a comport (C 91) or filled the center of a gothic arch (C 92). The Ideal Cut Glass Company placed a Russian border around a floral center (C 93). Certainly no pattern proved more popular. A few companies substituted other names for Russian but cut the same pattern. Mt. Washington Glass Works illustrated the pattern in a catalog as both Russian and Number 60. Wilcox Silver Plate Company eliminated the center star on the base of bowls, trays, or jugs and called the design Star and Hobnail. In spite of different names the pattern remained the same. A number of companies continued to identify the design as the Russian Pattern in spite of changes.

C 91. A comport (6.5 D x 5 H) with dominant motifs of hobstars and Russian.

C 92. A decanter (13 H) contained the Russian Pattern inside the gothic arches.

S 94. A comport (9 D x 6 H) cut in the Strawberry-Diamond Pattern.

S 93. A tray (12 D) cut by Ideal Cut Glass Company placed a Russian border around the flowers in the center.

STRAWBERRY-DIAMOND

In the basic Strawberry-Diamond Pattern rows of diamonds slanted from the base to the top. From the four sides of the diamonds short miters intersected to form a cross (S 94). In the best patterns the diamonds in the rows measured the same size. A number of companies trained apprentices cutting this pattern; consequently irregularities in the size of the diamonds do occur. Always check the diamonds for quality in size.

1. Fan Addition

Pattern designers soon added fans at the border of a piece (S 95). The fans consisted of five, seven, or nine prongs, depending on the size of cut glass piece. When the Strawberry-Diamond and Fan appeared on large pieces, someone misnamed the pattern "Pineapple and Fan" (S 96).

S 95. A comport (8 D x 5.5 H) cut in the Strawberry-Diamond and Fan Pattern.

2. Motifs

The Strawberry-Diamond pattern proved popular both as a major and minor motif. Hawkes and Libbey placed a diamond-shape frame around the crosscut diamond for a major motif. In a Hawkes pattern upper and lower fans separated the framed major motif. Libbey alternated the crosscut diamond with a crosshatched one in the Harvard Pattern (S 97).

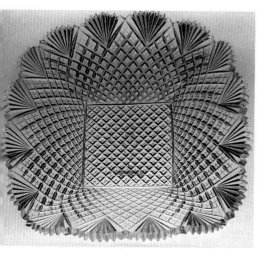

S 96. A square bowl (12 D x 6 H) some misname Pineapple-Diamond and Fan.

S 97. A finger bowl (4.5 D x 2.5 H) in Harvard Pattern by Libbey uses the crosscut diamond as a major motif.

Most of these patterns used a single star on the base (S 98). Some shapes, such as a tray (S 99) or a nappy (S 100), cut the base in the Strawberry-Diamond motif. Late in the Brilliant Period one company used Strawberry-Diamond to form a top and bottom border (S 101). This motif frequently appeared as a minor motif to cover small spaces in an ornate pattern. Throughout the forty years all companies cut stemware in Strawberry-Diamond and Fan (102). The pattern often proved a first choice with some companies for small pieces, such as a toothpick holder (S 103) or individual salts (S 104).

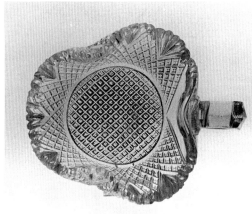

S 100. The Strawberry-Diamond covers the entire nappy.

S 98. A Roman punch cup (3 D x 2 H) contains a single star center.

S 101. A late ice tub (7 D x 8 H) has two borders of Strawberry-Diamond Pattern.

S 99. A tray (10 x 5) completely covered by the Strawberry-Diamond and Fan Pattern.

S 102. Most companies cut goblets in the Strawberry-Diamond and Fan Pattern.

S 103. A toothpick holder (2 D x 3 H) in the Strawberry-Diamond & Fan Pattern.

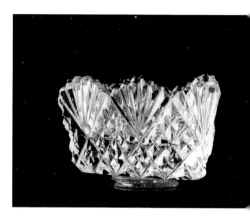

S 104. An individual salt in the Strawberry-Diamond and Fan Pattern.

PRISM PATTERNS

The Prism Pattern consisted of parallel, vertical miters that covered the entire blank. This early simplicity of the general cutting did not compete with other cut glass patterns, so companies tried to make the design more attractive.

1. Notching

To make the pattern more complicated, the master craftsman placed a simple notch on the vertical miters. Simple notching on the miters did not attract buyers. One company separated the notched prisms with clear panels and added sterling silver to rim and foot (D 105). Other companies varied the type of notching on each prism (S 106).

C 105. A vase (5 D x 9 H) cut with notched prisms and embellished with a sterling silver rim and foot.

S 106. A syrup (3 D x 6 H) has a notched prism pattern.

2. Geometric Additions

As previously mentioned, the craftsman added a horizontal border at the top consisting of different geometric motifs, such as stars and fans. Both Hawkes and Sinclaire placed such borders at both the top and bottom, using the decorated miters to unite the pattern. These changes inspired others to split the prisms with a center band of crosshatched motifs in framed diamonds (S 107). Next the artisan divided the prisms with a center band of stars and crosshatching (S 108). For contrast vertical prisms formed alternating panels on a vase topped with a border of 8-point stars (C 109).

S 109. A vase (5 D x 8.5 H) where notched prisms form a panel.

S 107. Candlesticks (14 H) with a center border between the notched prisms.

S 108. A jug (8 D x 8.5 H) divides the prism in half with a border.

3. Motifs

On a low bowl a grouping of notched prisms served as the major motif (S 110). The pattern of another bowl (S 111) combined with hobstars to form the linking motifs between large hobstars. Notched miters topped the combination motifs between buzzstars (S 112). On a sugar and cream (S 113) hobstars and triangles of crosshatching formed a top border for the notched miters. Notched prisms decorated the neck of a vase (C 114).

S 110. Notched miters form the major motifs on a bowl (8 D x 3.5 H).

C 111. Miters combine with stars to form a dominant, dual motif.

S 112. In a pattern cut on a bowl (8 D x 3.5 H) notched miters combined to form a dual motif.

S 113. A medium sized sugar and cream has a border above the notched miters.

C 114. Notched miters decorate the neck of a vase (7.5 D x 11.5 H).

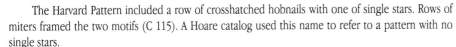

C 115. A cake tray (9 D) in a row pattern of Harvard.

HARVARD PATTERN

The Harvard Pattern included a row of crosshatched hobnails with one of single stars. Rows of miters framed the two motifs (C 115). A Hoare catalog used this name to refer to a pattern with no single stars.

Mt. Washington replaced the single star with an 8-point one and called the pattern Three Cut Octagon. This same company duplicated the Harvard Pattern, but named it Two Cut Octagon. Hawkes deleted the stars entirely and cut only the crosshatched hobnail in Pattern #3708 (C 116).

FADING PATTERNS

Some patterns that covered the entire blank disappeared early in the Brilliant Period.

1. Block Pattern

In the Block Pattern perpendicular and horizontal miters intersected to form a raised block (S 117). Both Mt. Washington and Dorflinger cut the Block Pattern in the early years of the Brilliant Period. Even with some variation the pattern lacked appeal for the public. The Boston and Sandwich Glass Company added a star to the block motif and even produced it in color-cut-to-clear. Nothing seemed to save it. For a short time Hoare used it as a minor motif.

C 116. A cologne (6.5 H) with crosshatched hobnails and no stars on Pattern #3708 by Hawkes.

S 117. Goblet in the Block Diamond Pattern by Mt. Washington.

S 118. A carafe (6.5 H) cut in the Sharp Diamond Pattern.

2. Sharp Diamond

This sharp, pointed diamond cut in diagonal rows lost it's points (S 118) and became the crosscut diamond. Early in the Brilliant Period a few companies cut it as a minor motif.

3. Hob Diamond or Hexagon Diamond

This pattern contained rows of clear diamonds with four sides (S 119). Some companies cut the Hob Diamond with six sides. Toward the turn of the century companies occasionally cut it as a minor motif.

4. Flute

The Flute Pattern, usually clear, consisted of straight or swirling panels (C 120). Hawkes, Clark, and Libbey cut this pattern for only a short time. Clark and Hawkes produced it in color-cut-to-clear designs. The flutes became a favorite way to decorate the necks of decanters (S 121), oils (S 122), and lips of jugs (P 123).

5. Clear Ovals

In an early pattern Dorflinger separated two rows of clear ovals with a deep miter. The company early ceased showing the pattern in the catalog. Pairpoint did cut a similar pattern but soon abandoned it.

By no means does this provide all the information on changes in early patterns of cut glass. This information does alert you to important changes from the original design and in some cases helps you approximate a date of cutting and possibly identify the source and name of a pattern.

C 119. A carafe (6.5 H) with matching tumbler in Hob Diamond Pattern by Dorflinger.

C 120. A jug (12 H) with sterling silver top cut in flutes that swirl.

C 121. A decanter (5 D x 13 H) has notched flutes cut on the neck.

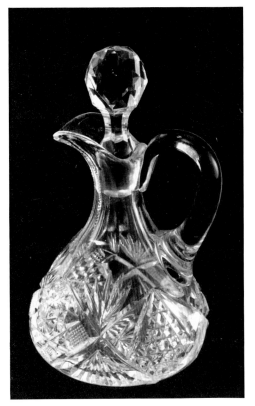

S 122. Flutes cut on the neck of an oil.

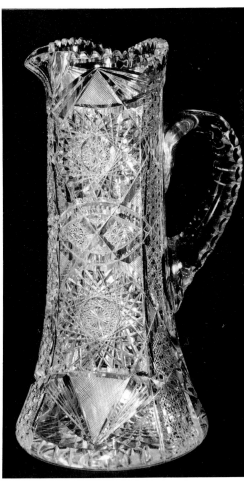

C 123. Flutes cut on the lip of a jug (7.5 x 14 H).

Before you buy a piece of cut glass, quickly check it for extra value. Extra value refers to any addition beyond the standard shape. Most companies cut some pieces in standard shapes, such as a decanter (C 124) or a bowl (C 125). Any time a shape added a foot or a handle, for example, to a standard shape, the value increased. A piece with such additions, most likely, will hold the price you paid or increase in value. So check any cut glass pieces for these extra values.

STOPPERS

A stopper consists of three parts: a head, neck, and insert. Changes in any of these parts could affect the value. Of primary importance, the stopper needs to fit the neck and go with the shape as pictured in old cut glass catalogs.

1. Original or Replacement

Sometimes a wrong stopper gets put with a shape--a marriage rather than the original mate. Since American companies made standard-size necks and stoppers, you may get a married replacement. Feel inside the neck of a stoppered piece for a slight ridge. If the stopper sits above (C 126) or below this ridge, someone has performed a marriage. Now move the stopper back and forth to see if it rocks. The correct stopper fits tightly in the neck.

Next see if the size of the stopper looks right for the shape--not too large or too small. The shape needs to match the piece as shown in old catalogs, discussed in more detail later.

Companies purposely ground both the insert of the stopper and the neck to keep the contents air tight. These shapes include colognes, smelling salt bottles, and tobacco jars, to name a few. If the piece has only the stopper insert or the inner neck ground, someone has put them together.

Occasionally companies put a number on the neck of the shape and a matching one on the side or base of the stopper. If you find these matching numbers, most likely you have the original stopper.

C 124. A standard shape for a decanter (12 H) in a dual
motif outline that adds value.

C 125. A low bowl (8 D x 2 H) in a standard star outline that
provided for a more ornate pattern.

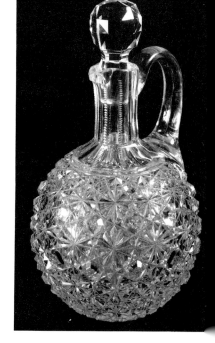

C 126. A whiskey jug (4.5 D x 8 H) in the Russian Pattern has an
incorrectly shaped stopper that does not fit the neck.

2. Lapidary Stopper

With the lapidary stopper, companies decorated the round head with multi-cut, clear facets. This standard stopper with a long, fluted neck mated with a standard decanter or with an oil (C 127). Hawkes occasionally substituted a slightly pointed top on the usually round facet stopper. This small change did not really affect the value.

Companies added extra value to a long neck stopper by replacing the lapidary head with one that matched the pattern on the shape (C 128). Hoare added more value by not only matching the pattern on the shape but topping it with a facet cut, round knob (C 129). A stopper in an unidentified decanter flattened the round shape, kept the faceted half knob at the top but added a full knob to the long stem (C 130). No doubt you can find other deviations from the standard on long neck stoppers.

C 129. A stopper with a decanter (5.5 D x 12.5 H) in the Naples Pattern by Hoare not only matched the pattern but added a partial knob on top for more value.

C 127. The stoppers of these two oils fit their necks perfectly.

C 128. The stopper on this decanter (13 H) matched the pattern on the shape.

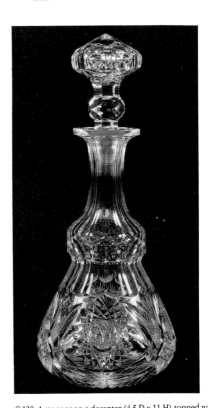

C 130. A stopper on a decanter (4.5 D x 11 H) topped with a full knob and another facet cut knob on the neck for added value.

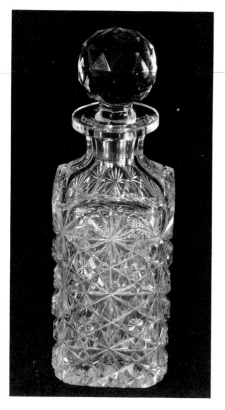

C 131. A cologne in the Russian Pattern with a round, facet stopper.

S 132. A short neck stopper on a catsup bottle (7.5 H) with a single star cut on top for more value.

S 133. A horseradish bottle (3 D x 5 H) has a single star on top to increase the value.

The lapidary stopper with a short neck went with such shapes as colognes (C 131), whiskey jugs, or catsup bottles. To add a plus value to a short neck stopper of a catsup bottle, a company cut a deep single star on the top (S 132). Normally companies decorated a hollow stopper on a horseradish bottle (S 133) or one for cherries (S 134) with some form of cutting. An undecorated top on these may indicate the wrong stopper. An ornate, sterling silver stopper always added a note of elegance and value (C 135).

S 134. A decorated, hollow stopper on a cherry bottle (3.5 D x 6 H) made it more valuable.

C 135. A sterling silver stopper on a cologne (5 H) added value.

3. Tall Pointed Stoppers

Americans placed the tall, pointed stopper with a short neck on wine bottles (C 136). The standard stopper usually contained clear panels.

Some companies decorated the clear panels to make the stopper more ornate. The craftsman sometimes slightly rounded the pointed top and added step cutting or panels of crosshatching (C 137). For extra value a flute decoration enlarged the base of the head but kept the paneled point (C 138).

4. Cylindrical Stopper

The cylindrical stopper consisted of a clear head with a flat top and no neck (C 139). Companies put this type of stopper on a tall whiskey bottle or a squat whiskey jug. As patterns on shapes became more decorative, the craftsmen cut the rim of this stopper with prisms, clear panels, or crosshatching.

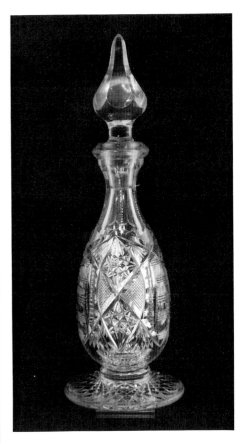

C 138. A pointed stopper on this wine bottle (9 H) consisted of panels that narrow to a point at top.

C 139. A cylinder stopper on a whiskey bottle (12.5 H) has a flat top and matches the neck.

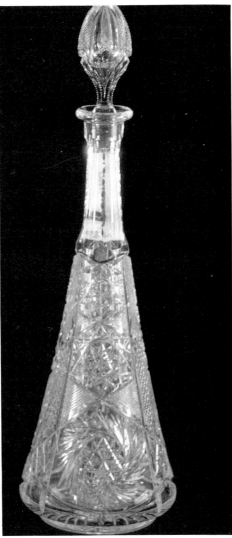

C 137. The pointed stopper on a wine bottle (16 H) contained an extra with crosshatched panels.

C 136. A pointed stopper with facets on a wine bottle (13 H) showed extra value.

S 140. A Worcestershire bottle (8 H) with a flat topped stopper contains a decorated edge.

5. Flat Top Stopper

The flat top stopper went on tall, circular colognes or Worcestershire bottles (S 140). This flat stopper with a thin shape contained a short fluted neck. The edge of the stopper may remain clear or contain a simple cutting of parallel miters.

Craftsmen found ways to elaborate this flat stopper. They cut a design on the top or made the edges more ornate with flutes, ovals, or diamonds. With more cutting on patterns companies even changed the thin edge around the top to a rounded one with flutes and decorated the top with a single star (C 141).

When you attend antiques shows, museum displays, or any cut glass exhibit, notice the stoppers. You may see a unique whiskey bottle in which the stopper repeats the shape (C 142). Stoppers offered companies many opportunities to add extra value to pieces of cut glass.

C 141. A Worcestershire bottle (2.5 D x 8 H) has a stopper decorated with flutes.

C 142. The stopper on a whiskey bottle (4.5 D x 10.5 H) repeated the hour-glass shape of the item for value.

FOOTED PIECES

A foot consisted of a base and a stem. Some pieces, such as a comport (C 143), stemware (S 144), or plain candlesticks, contained a foot as part of the standard shape. The standard shape of bowls, relishes, or jugs included no foot. By adding a foot to a relish (C 145) or an orange bowl (C 146), craftsmen gave these pieces extra value.

C 143. The basic shape for a comport (5 D x 5 H).

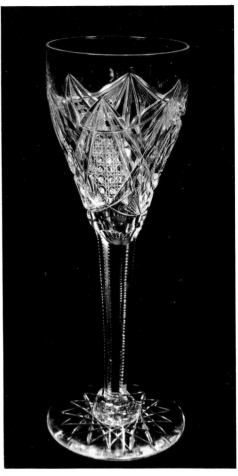

S 144. A Rhine wine (4.5 D x 11 H) in a basic shape that included a foot.

C 145. The addition of a foot to a relish dish (6.5 D x 4 H) increased the value.

C 146. A foot on an orange bowl (9 x 7 x 6.5 H) raised the value.

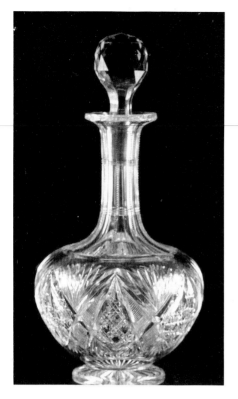

C 147. The addition of a base only to a decanter (12 H) still increased the value.

C 148. A base on a jug (4.5 D x 15 H) added value.

P 149. A foot on a jug (5.5 D x 14 H) made the piece more valuable.

1. Base

Companies did not need to add the entire foot to increase the value. In some examples, they achieved extra value by adding only a base to a standard shape that did not include a foot, such as a decanter (C 147) or a jug (C 148).

Do examine the cutting on the base. The standard base contained a radial or single star. A few bases displayed a flashed star. A hobstar cut on the base of a jug (P 149) or a scollop around its edge (P 150) showed value. Other decorations on a base included cane, Strawberry-Diamond, or bars of cross-hatching. On candlesticks in a thistle pattern, the artisan repeated the floral design around the top edge of the base (S 151). Sinclaire often added a floral border around the base edge.

Companies usually signed on top or under the edge of the base. This raised the value because a signature identifies the company that produced the cut glass piece.

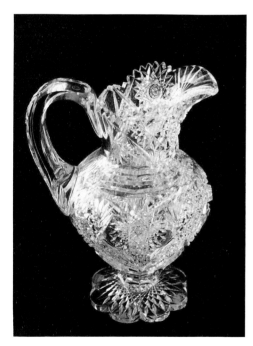

P 150. A scalloped foot on this jug (7 D x 10 H) raised the value.

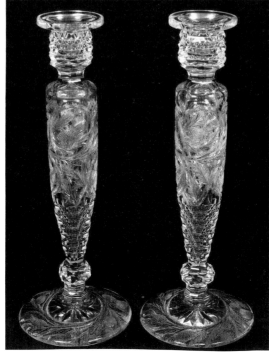

S 151. The value increased on a candlestick holder (12 H) that repeated the thistle design on the top rim of the foot.

C 152. The hobstar on the foot of a dish (5.5 x 3.5 x 4 H)
made the piece more valuable.

2. Stem

The height of the stem measured either short or tall. A short, clear stem on a relish (S 152) or a sugar and cream set (S 153) added somewhat to the value. A slightly taller stem with notched flutes on an upright celery holder (C 154) or a fan-shaped vase (C 155) makes these pieces more valuable.

The stems of vases also underwent more ornamentation. One vase contained a faceted knob on the stem near the base (P 156). In another vase the pattern on the ball matched that on the shape (P 157) for a raise in value.

S 153. A short foot on a sugar and cream set added some value.

C 154. A footed celery (9.5 H) provided more value with notched panels.

C 155. The value on this fan-shaped vase depended on the height and the decoration on the foot.

Tall stems offered more opportunity for embellishment. A clear stem on a relish may display only notched panels (S 158) or a slight bulge on a comport for a teardrop (C 159). More ornate stems on comports included two interlocking ones (S 160) or Saint Louis diamonds (C 161). Certain goblets contained faceted knobs under the cup, near the base, or at both the top and base of the stem.

Several companies applied peg feet to standard shapes with no feet. Such applications included a sugar and cream (C 162), a whip cream bowl (C 163), a tall vase (P 164), and a 9-inch bowl (C 165). Another deviation on a foot included a conical one on a comport or a candlestick (C 166).

C 156. A faceted knob at the base provided a plus value on this vase (8 D x 12 H).

S 158. A notched panel stem and flashed star on the base made this footed relish more valuable.

C 159. A comport (6.5 D x 9.5 H) gained a plus with a teardrop in the stem.

P 157. A knob at the base matched the pattern on this two part vase (12 H) with a Russian Pattern cut on the foot.

S 160. A twisted stem on this comport improved the value.

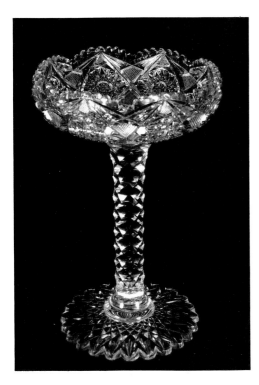

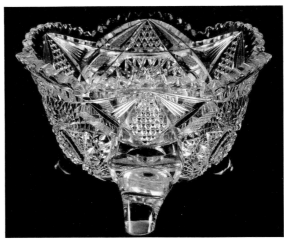

C 163. A whipped cream bowl (7.5 D x 4.5 H) improved in
value with the peg feet.

C 161. A St. Louis diamond stem along with the hobstar
base made this comport (12 H) worth more.

P 164. A vase (16.5 H) gained in value with peg feet.

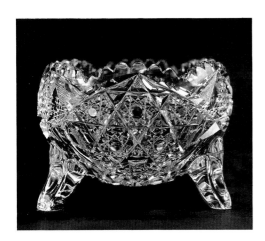

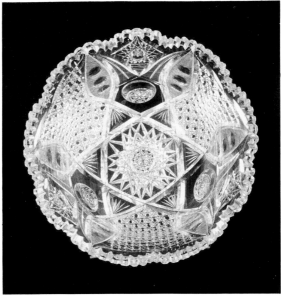

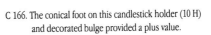

C 165. A bowl (9 D) increased in value with decorated, peg
feet.

C 166. The conical foot on this candlestick holder (10 H)
and decorated bulge provided a plus value.

C 162. Peg feet raised the value on this medium-size sugar
and cream set.

C 167. A jug (10 H) has a standard handle.

HANDLES

Certain shapes in cut glass normally contained an applied handle as standard equipment. These include jugs (C 167), sugar and cream (C 168), ice bowls, and loving cups (C 169). An increase in value occurred when pieces usually with handles contained none as in a sugar and cream set (C 170) or a Roman punch cup. Companies shaped a built-in handle on a shell shaped bonbon (S 171) or an ice tub (S 172).

1. Number of Handles

In one old catalog the company offered to add a handle for an extra fee to a matching saucer for a bowl or a plate for an ice cream tray. Frequently, these special pieces get mistaken for a nappy or a handled plate. The saucer measures 4.5 or 5 inches in diameter as compared to six inches or more for a nappy or plate. A few collectors give the saucer and plate a higher evaluation than the nappy because of the scarcity. The price of the nappy rises with the number of handles, such as one (S 173), two (C 174), or three, the one with the greatest value.

Companies added handles to other pieces that normally contained none for an increase in value. The craftsman applied two handles to an upright spooner (C 175), a mayonnaise set (C 176), or an upright celery.

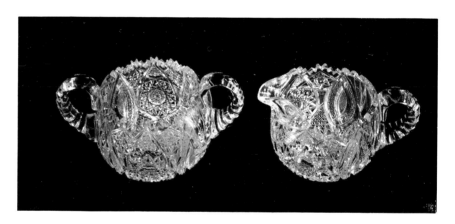

C 168. Cut handles on a medium-sized sugar and cream increased the value.

C 169. The signature of Sinclaire added more value than the thumbprints on the handles of this loving cup.

C 170. The lack of handles on a medium-sized sugar provides more value.

S 171. The built-in handle on a shell bonbon (5 x 6) did not increase the value.

C 174. A two handled nappy (9.5 D) with crimped edge.

S 172. An ice tub (8 D) with built-in handles depended more on the pattern for value.

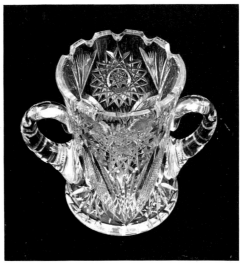

C 175. The company added two handles to this upright spoonholder (3 D x 5 H) for a value increase.

C 176. Two notched handles decorated those on the bowl (3.5 D x 7 H) of a mayonnaise set for more value.

S 173. A nappy (6 D) with one handle.

C 177. A typically applied handle on a jug (8.5 H).

2. Location of Handles

On standard pieces, as a jug (C 177), a basket (C 178), or a sugar bowl (C 179), the craftsman applied handles at almost the same places, near the edge at the top and along the side.

The handle on a butter receiver or a ring tree always placed the handle in the center. Since the standard shapes of these pieces followed almost the same placement from piece to piece, these handles usually do not affect the value.

The placement of handles can change the value. For example, on one vase the handles begin level with the top edge, an unusual place (C 180) or with another at the indentation of the neck (C 181). A curved handle in the center of heart-shaped bonbons (S 182) and (S 183) get a value increase because the second one contained a Libbey signature. Pitkin and Brooks placed a handle for a relish on an indented side. The limited production of many of these special pieces, nevertheless, provided as much extra value as the handle placement.

C 179. Applied handles on a sugar bowl (5.5 D x 7 H) began close to the top edge.

C 178. On a basket (7 D x 6 H) the applied handles began at the top rim.

C 180. Applied handles on a vase (10.5 x 9 H) began even
with the top.

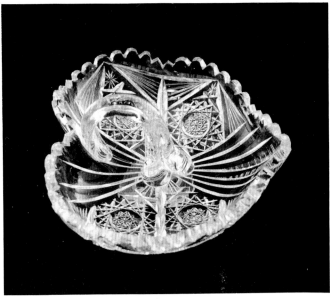

S 182. An applied center handle typical of a heart shaped
bonbon, but Libbey signature also increased the
value.

C 181. Handles on this vase (8 D x 15.5 H) started at the
indented neck for added value.

S 183. A curved center handle on a heart bonbon (5 x 5)
supplied the raised value.

C 184. The odd application of the handle on this jug (5 D x 7 H) suggested a raise in value.

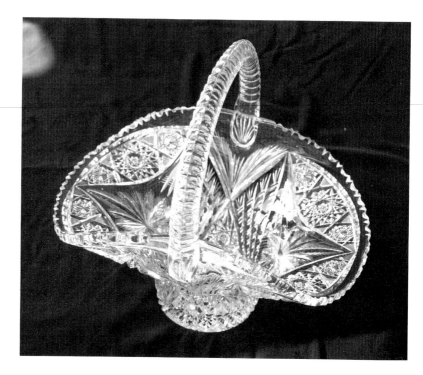

C 186. The honeycombed handle and the oval shape on this basket added the value.

3. Decorations on the Handle

At the beginning of the Brilliant Period, the applied handles contained no decoration. As patterns became more ornate, companies replaced the clear, rounded handles with flat sides for decorating. Decorations included single thumbprints on the handle of one jug (C 184) and double ones (C 185), or honeycomb on the handle of a basket (C 186). A number of companies did not stop with thumbprints but decorated handles on jugs with rings (C 187) and crosshatching on a handle of a nappy cut in Strawberry-Diamond and Fan (S 188).

C 187. The heavily cut handle and the sterling silver on the neck of this tanker (6 D x 11.5 H) provided the increased value.

C 185. The honeycombed handle on this jug (11.5 H) showed a basic placement.

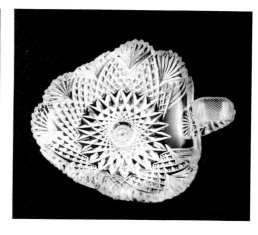

S 188. The crosshatching on top of the handle of this bonbon in Strawberry-Diamond and Fan added a plus.

DECORATED NECKS

The basic decorations on a neck of a cut glass piece follows, more or less, the standard designs. The neck of a jug contains plain flutes (S 189) or notched panels (C 190). Stair steps decorated the neck of a flower center (C 191). You can easily recognize these cuttings. As with other shapes in cut glass, necks of standard shapes became more decorative with embellished patterns.

The honeycombed neck of a pepper sauce bottle went exceptionally well with the sterling silver stopper (S 192). The most decorative neck on a wine bottle consisted of notched panels and an applied neck ring. (C 193). A decorated neck gave a better grip on the item. On a decanter the craftsman may place a single decorative neck ring (C 194). Some companies did not stop with one but cut three. The decoration on the ring ranged from simple facets to ornate motifs.

Rather than apply decorated rings, the blower of blanks bulged the neck (C 195). Two decanters contained two bulges decorated with flutes (C 196). One designer added a decoration to a single bulge to imitate a neck ring (C 197).

These identifications of extra values only provide a basis for adding others as you shop for more valuable cut glass pieces to add to your collection.

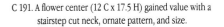

C 191. A flower center (12 C x 17.5 H) gained value with a stairstep cut neck, ornate pattern, and size.

S 189. This standard jug in Strawberry-Diamond and Fan has a notched panel neck for more value.

C 190. The shape, the pattern, and the notched flutes on this jug (11 H) added the value.

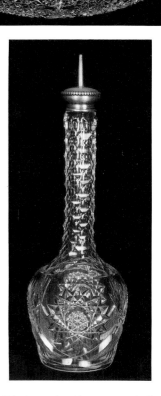

S 192. Value increased on this pepper sauce bottle with the honeycombed neck and sterling silver stopper.

C 193. A neck ring on this wine bottle (14 H) made it more valuable.

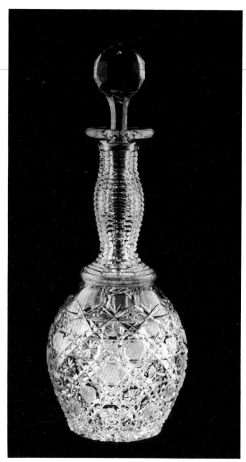

C 195. The rings on the bulged neck of this decanter (14 H), along with the stopper that matched the pattern, raised the value.

C 196. A decorated bulge on the neck of the decanters (12 H) suggested an increase in value.

C 197. Note the neck ring on the bulge of the decanter.

C 194. This decanter gained value with a decorated neck ring and a handle.

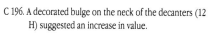

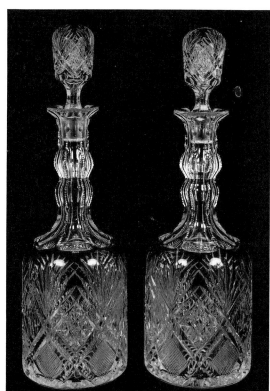

CHAPTER 5 *The Factual And The Fanciful*

In recent years new descriptions of old cut glass can blur rather than improve communications between seller and buyer. An understanding of the intended meaning of these fanciful expressions and a comparison of them to the limited descriptions in old catalogs can improve communication, and, most likely, correct any misconceptions. Certainly a merger of the two can result in better relations between the collector and the dealer.

LARGE SHAPES OF OLD CUT GLASS

Old catalogs provided little or no description for old cut glass shapes. They identified the function, named the pattern, and stated the size. For containers of liquids the catalog usually listed the capacity. The picture actually completed the description. Yet the catalogs do give the basis for building a successful merger.

1. Baskets

The catalogs identified these shapes for baskets: bonbon, flower, and basket. A bonbon basket consisted of a small round shape with a very shallow depth (C 198) and a tall one as a flower basket (C 199). The one in between the two sizes the catalog simply designated a basket (P 200).

C 199. A flower basket (12.5 D x 18 H).

C 198. A bonbon basket (8 D).

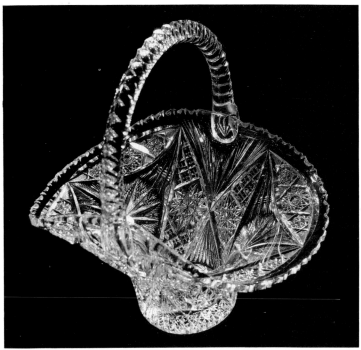

P 200. A basket (13.5 D x 10.5 H).

C 201. No one could explain the name of the "helmet" basket (6 x 3).

C 202. A descriptive term of "rope" handle on a basket (9 D x 5.5 H).

The new description of "daffodil" basket obviously refers to the catalog's flower basket. No one could explain the meaning of a "helmet" basket (C 201) with an oval shape.

Baskets contained a curved handle, but no catalogs mentioned this feature. Perhaps the curved handle rated as standard equipment.

Evidently the present-day describer considered some types of handles worthy of mention. A double handle twisted together became a "rope" handle (C 202).

2. Bowls

Companies produced several shapes in bowls. Generally catalogs identified a basic bowl as round or salad (C 203) and gave the diameter as 8, 9, and 10 inches. The addition of a foot--not a standard--the catalogs called footed bowl.

The new description calls this size and shape a "berry" bowl. A foot on a 10-bowl converts it to an "ambrosia" bowl.

The catalogs identified a deep, oval bowl with pointed ends as a fruit bowl (P 204). If the company added a foot, it became a fancy fruit bowl. In the same trend a large, round bowl with a turned over rim (not turned down or curved), companies, such as Pairpoint, called a flower bowl.

C 203. A round or salad bowl (9 D x 3.5 H).

P 204. A fruit bowl (6 x 12).

P 205. A fruit bowl (9 x 14) with the improvised names of
"banana" or "Napoleon's Hat."

Since the oval fruit bowl seemed to easily fit the shape of a banana, someone assigned it the name of "banana" bowl. Another person visualized the shape as a "Napoleon's Hat" (P 205). The large rounded bowl with a turned over rim became a "bishop's hat" or a "lady's spittoon."

Most catalogs illustrate two types of punch bowls: with or without a foot (C 206). Under the illustration, some catalogs added foot meaning a conical foot (C 206). In a few catalogs, you will find an illustration of a comport punch bowl (P 207). You could use the two parts separately: the foot as a comport or vase and the top as a bowl.

The new descriptions tried to give punch bowls more specific functions by referring to them as "Tom and Jerry," "eggnog," or "wassail". A covered punch bowl received the name of "syllabub" (P 208).

P 207. A comport punch bowl (12 D x 16 H).

C 206. A punch bowl (15 D x 13 H) with a conical foot.

P 208. A covered punch bowl (9 D x 16 H) to which someone applied the identification of "syllabub."

P 209. A typical decanter (16 H).

C 210. A whiskey decanter (12 H) with two whiskey
tumblers.

3. Decanters

According to the catalogs, a decanter consisted of a rounded body, long slender neck, and a stopper (P 209). The catalogs gave this shape no recognition for a decorated neck, an ornate pattern, or an added base. Several catalogs did identify a shorter, bulbous whiskey decanter (C 210).

The lack of description for shapes annoyed a few who added such visual terms as "bowling pin," "bell-like," or "footed" (S 211). The narrow ring that joins the foot to the body of the decanter received the name of "wafer" (C 212). A bulge in the neck earned the title of "goose neck" (C 213).

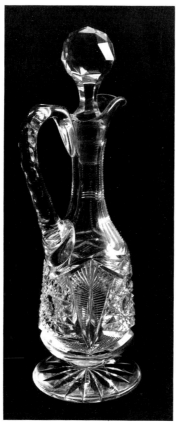

S 211. A "footed" decanter (3 D x 9 H).

C 212. A "wafer" on a decanter (4 D x 13 H) joined the base
with the liquid container.

C 215. A water jug (5.5 D x 8.5 H).

C 213. A decanter (5.5 D x 12 H) with a "goose" neck.

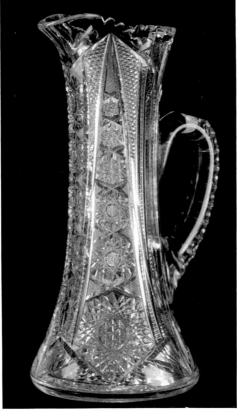

C 214. A tall jug called a tankard (13.5 H).

C 216. A descriptive name of "squat" jug (8.5 H).

C 217. An improvised term "bulbous jug" (6 D x 6.5 H).

4. Jugs

Most catalogs referred to a tall pitcher as a tankard jug (C 214). Several catalogs identified the function of the tankard to hold claret, wine, or champagne. Some catalogs called the tankard a Flemish jug. A few catalogs listed a smaller jug for water (C 215). Of course, illustrations in the catalogs showed jugs as squat (C 216) or bulbous (C 217) but gave them no description. Catalogs appeared more interested in stating the capacity of the jug. After the turn of the century a few companies, such as Straus or Taylor Brothers, used the term "pitcher." Even in the same catalog you find both references to the same shape as jug or pitcher.

Late describers felt the pitchers needed classification of function. So they designated a small pitcher for "milk" or "butter milk" (C 218) or a tankard for lemonade (C 219). A fancy jug with a low bulbous shape became a "petticoat" pitcher (C 220). Silver on the rim identified the piece as a "collared" pitcher (C 221). The catalogs listed none of these identifications.

C 218. A made-up function of "milk" or "buttermilk" jug (6.5 D x 7 H).

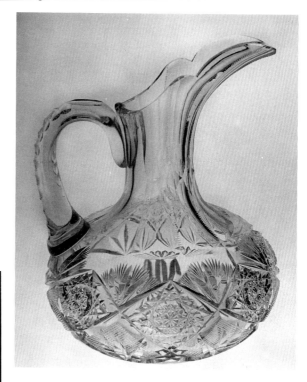

C 220. A "petticoat pitcher" (6 D x 8 H) signed by Hawkes.

C 219. A tankard (12 H) given an improvised function of "lemonade pitcher."

C 221 A tankard (15.5 H) with a silver rim designated a "collared pitcher."

5. Vases

Companies produced vases in numerous shapes, but the catalogs gave them no special names. A Quaker City catalog, the exception, referred to four vases as a revolving one in three parts, a globe shape, a cylinder one, and a fancy one, all heavily cut. Most catalogs did state the height of a vase.

Imaginative people thought the shape needed describing even though the catalogs did not. Certain shapes stirred the fancy of one who named it a "bowling pin" vase (C 222). "Hour Glass" described a vase that bulged at the top and bottom (C 223). A vase that bulged at the top, narrowed in the middle, widened at the lower part, and resembled the shape of a woman wearing a corset became a "corset" vase (C 224).

C 224. This vase (4 D x 10 H) acquired the description of a "corset" shape.

C 222. A vase (13 H) some call a "bowling pin" shape.

C 223. A vase (14 H) described as having an "hour glass" shape.

Any vase with a flared rim got identified as a "tulip"(C 225) or a "trumpet" vase (C 226). Since a number of vases stood eighteen to twenty-five inches tall, the fancy soared with the height. Such sizes received the name of "grand piano" vase (P 227). A tall cylinder vase became a "cane" or "umbrella" stand (P 228).

6. New Conceptions

A quick comparison of the catalog information with new conceptions in a single sentence easily increases your vision. A cake tray on a foot--not standard--may get identified as a "doughnut stand." An ice cream tray with two flared ends became a "fishtail" tray (P 229). Another person described a lamp as "Gone-with-the-Wind" because of the similar shape to one that appeared in that movie. A bread tray inspired the name "bun" tray.

A dome covered cheese someone designated a "cake server" (C 230). The shallow dish with handles and a dome cover holds mushrooms and not "caviar" (P 231). The catalogs list a round bowl with two built-in handles as an ice tub--not an "ice bucket" (C 232). A round bowl with applied handles and the addition of a separate drainer takes the catalog name of ice bowl--not bucket (C 233). That expensive "champagne bucket" with a liner several catalogs identify as a flower pot (C 234).

C 225. A description called this shape a "tulip" vase (11 H).

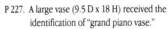

P 227. A large vase (9.5 D x 18 H) received the identification of "grand piano vase."

C 226. A vase (12 D x 20 H) some person saw as a "trumpet" shape.

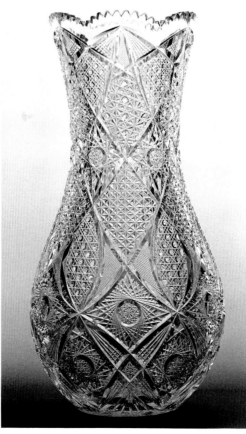

L 228. A vase (9 D x 25 H) the identifier called a "cane" or "umbrella" stand.

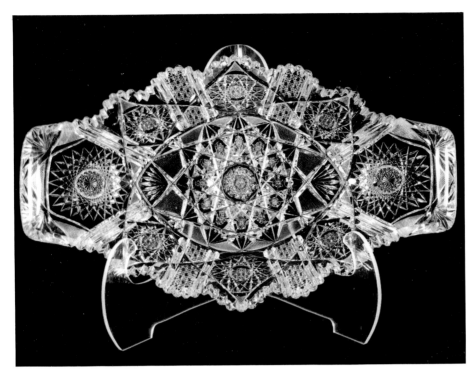

P 229. The spreading two ends of this shape (9.5 x 17) the
viewer saw as a "fishtail tray."

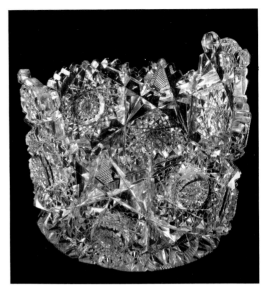

C 232. An ice tub (8 D x 4 H).

C 230. A covered cheese (8 D x 6 H) called a cake server
but not by a catalog.

C 233. An ice bowl (12 D x 8 H).

P 231. The catalogs call this dome covered dish (8 D x 6 H)
a mushroom holder.

C 234. A flower pot with a lining.

BORROWED TERMS

Borrowing terms provided one means of detailing the fancy image.

1. Modern Usage

The catalogs identified a large jar as a cracker jar (C 235); modern application calls it a "cookie" jar. Another modern term, "humidor," replaces what the catalogs called tobacco, cigarette, or cigar jars (C 236). These three jars contained a ground neck to make them air tight. A carafe with a tumbler on top the catalogs described was an eye opener, sick or guest room bottle, not a "tumble up." Catalogs pictured an oil (C 237) and not a "cruet" or a compote as a comport (L 238). Late in the Brilliant Period a few companies used the terms cruet and compote.

Puff box, the catalog term, someone called a "powder box." Since no modern term existed for a covered bonbon (S 239) as illustrated in catalogs, it got called a "collar holder" or a "casserole." A Roman punch cup (S 240), because it has no handles, the renamers called a "ramekin" or "custard cup."

C 235. A cracker jar (6 D x 9 H).

C 237. An oil (3 D x 6.5 H).

S 236. A cigar jar (4.5 D x 8 H).

L 238. A three part comport (12 D x 18 H).

S 239. A covered bonbon (8 D x 4 H).

S 240. A Roman punch cup.

2. Older Terms

Terms from the past find a place among the new identifications. A relish in the shape of a half moon by Hawkes became a "bone dish" (C 241). A small dresser jar became a "collar button holder" (S 242).

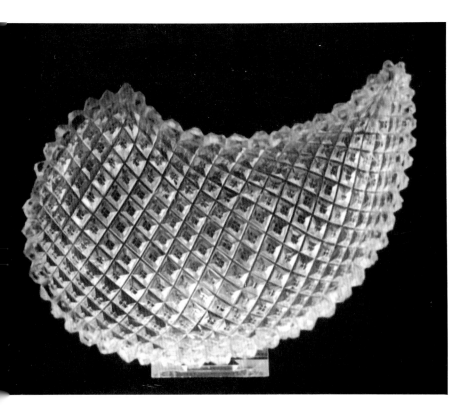

C 241. A bonbon in Strawberry-Diamond by Hawkes.

S 242. A dresser jar (3.5 D x 2 H).

C 244. A pointed oval motif on an oil (8 H).

C 243. A comport (8 H).

3. Foreign Terms

A few believed that calling a piece of cut glass by a foreign name added glamour. A comport, a v-shape bowl on a foot, received the name of "tazza vase" (C 243). For a pointed oval surrounding a group of minor motifs (C 244) the catalogs do not use the term "vesica". "Dentil" comes from Latin and refers to a sawtooth, but catalogs do not use it.

SMALL SHAPES

Small shapes do not get overlooked in the renaming.

1. Dining Room

The catalog identified a set shaped as a spade (C 245), heart, diamond, and club as bonbons and not a bridge set. People played the game of euchre and not bridge during the Brilliant Period. You can easily see why anyone would called a knife rest a "barbell" (C 246). A "stick dish" actually describes a bonbon with a center handle (S 247). An oval nut dish some visualized as an "almond oval." The shape described for a banana split the catalogs defined as a footed relish (S 248). Companies cut three sized of sugar and cream sets: small, medium, and large. Someone called the largest size a "boarding house" or "plantation" set.

C 245. A spade shape (8 x 8) in a euchre set or a bonbon.

C 246. A knife rest (5.5).

C 247. A bonbon (6 D).

S 248. A footed relish (6 D x 4 H).

2. Drinking Vessels

The catalogs listed a drinking vessel as a mug and not a stein. Do use the catalog term whiskey tumbler (S 249) rather than the new one of "double shot glass". A champagne tumbler (S 250) the catalogs did list but no "juice" glass. The goblet that flares at the rim the catalogs labeled an ice tea glass and not a "lemonade" or "tulip" goblet. The catalogs do not use the term "supreme" for a footed punch cup. The improviser identified a pepper sauce bottle (C 251) as a barber bottle.

S 250. A champagne tumbler (2 D x 3.5 H).

S 249. A whiskey tumbler (2.5 D x 3 H).

C 251. A pepper sauce bottle.

3. Personal Usage

Catalogs do picture a lady's flask and not a "lay down perfume bottle" (S 252). The old term smelling salt bottle received the new description, "perfume dispenser" (C 253). The long round bottle with a ventilated top according to the catalogs referred to a tooth brush bottle or holder—not a "pungent" bottle. Catalogs described the small round dish with a handle and place for a candle in the center (signed Hawkes) as a candlestick holder (C 254)—not a chamberstick.

S 252. Two lady's flasks (2.5 x 4) and (3 x 5.5).

S 253. A smelling salts bottle (3 H).

C 254. A candlestick holder signed Hawkes.

FANCIFUL IMAGES

The imaginative created fanciful images to provide sharper descriptions for pieces of cut glass. The fanciful may apply to the entire shape or only a part.

1. Extra Additions

Handles on a loving cup with silver by Shreve began large near the base and gradually grew smaller, so someone visualized the shape as "elephant tusks" (C 255). A visualizer saw the shape of the handles on an ice bowl as "elephant ears" (C 256). A jug handle decorated with hobnails became a "button" handle. Two knobs on either end of a stem that joined the cup and the base of a champagne became an "apple core" stem (C 257). A cylindrical stopper with parallel notched miters suggested a "corn cob" stopper.

2. Edges or Rims

Generally, catalogs show pieces of cut glass with a straight, sawtooth, or scalloped sawtooth edge. Late in the Brilliant Period companies used a straight edge to reduce costs. Clark cut the scalloped rim like a stairway, but someone saw it as a "castle" edge (C 258). The catalogs referred to a rim that goes in and out as crimped (P 259), but it has become known as a "blown out" edge.

C 257. A champagne (8 H) with an "apple core" stem.

C 255. A loving cup (5.5 D x 7 H) with handles shaped like "elephant tusks", a description. A Shreve hallmark on the silver.

C 258. A "castle rim" on a plate by Clark in Prima Donna Pattern.

C 256. An ice bowl (10 D x 6 H) according to a describer has handles like "elephant ears."

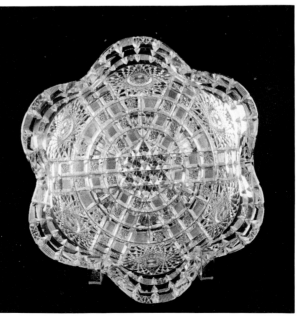

P 259. A bowl (10 D) with a crimped rim.

C 260. A bowl (8 D x 3.5 H) with a flashed star motif.

C 262. A bowl (8 D x 3.5 H) with a feathered star motif.

3. Motifs

Personal interviews with old cutters and descendants provided the names for both major and minor motifs. Not satisfied with the mundane names for motifs, someone decided to make the descriptions more graphic. A flashed star (C 260) took the name of "Florence" star, the same star Libbey used in the Florence pattern. The sunburst motif (S 261) received the descriptive name of "bull's eye", and a blazed star became a "lacy" star (C 262). A swirling panel (P 263) some person saw as a "swag."

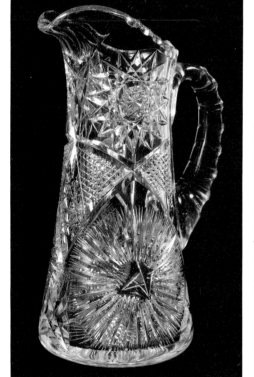

S 261. A bowl (11 D x 3.5 H) with a sunburst motif.

P 263. A bowl (10 D x 4.5 H) an unknown person called a
    "swag" pattern.

S 264. A jar hallmarked by Tiffany and cut in a notched prism pattern.

S 266. A spoon holder (6 H) with a "bow tie" minor motif.

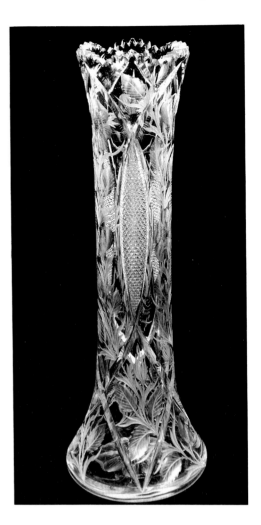

C 268. A vase (5.5 D x 16 H) used a minor motif of pointed diamonds.

Minor motifs offered equal opportunities for new fancies. The catalogs notched prism (S 264) receive the identity of "zipper," "punt beading," or "notched ribs." A notched flute became a "prism throat." Crosshatching from the catalogs (S 265) identified as "nail file," "satin lines," "crisscross," or "window screen." A "bow tie" motif (S 266) consisted of two triangles of crosshatching meeting at one point. Other renaming of catalog minor motifs included "chair bottom" for cane (C 267), "grid" for nail head diamond (C 268), "diagonal ribs" for fans (S 269), and "lattice" for step cutting on a footed bowl (C 270).

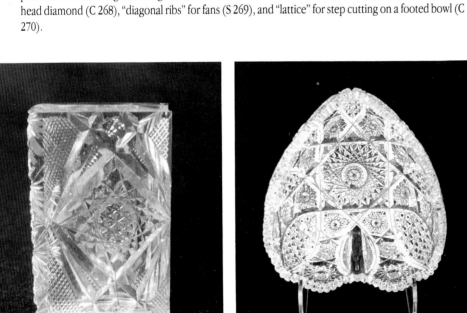

C 267. A heart shaped tray (8 x 9 x 3.5) has minor motifs of cane.

S 265. A paper weight (3 x 4.5) with crosshatched minor motifs.

S 269. A low bowl (8 D x 2 H) contained a fan border.

C 270. A footed bowl (10 D x 9 H) with step cutting on the base.

S 271. A violet vase (3.5 D x 4 H).

4. Miniatures or Salesman Samples

Companies used catalogs for orders, and salesmen did not carry small samples around according to interviews we have made with people associated with glass production. The imaginative person, however, matched smaller pieces to shapes of larger ones and proclaimed them miniatures. A violet vase became a miniature flower center (S 271). Individual salts get renamed as ice tubs (S 272), a master salt as a stamp moistener (S 273), or as a two handled bowl (S 274). An individual olive dish identified as a miniature celery (S 275).

S 272. An individual salt (2 D x 1.5 H).

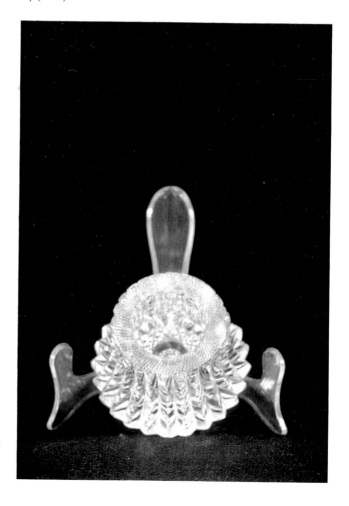

S 273. A master salt (3 D x 2 H).

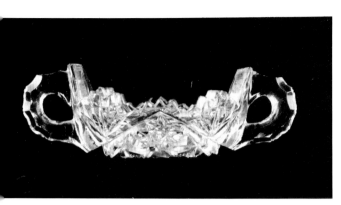

S 274. An individual salt (2.5 D x 1 H) with handles.

S 275. An individual olive dish (3 x 6).

5. Challenges

Some fanciful descriptions prove difficult to related to old catalogs. A pattern called a "Picket Fence" may refer to the Renaissance or Block Pattern. A "baluster" piece may mean a pattern cut in prisms. A lamp with a "coolie shade" and signed Fry describes a round shade with a pointed top (P 276). Incidently, catalogs did not show a ginger or apothecary jar.

By no means does this discussion contain all descriptions. No doubt you know these and others. Any time that these new descriptions make communication more visual, by all means use them. Try to merge the old with the new so you have the best of both.

P 276. A lamp (13 H) signed Fry.

85,907. CUT-GLASS RECEPTACLE. CARL V. HELMSCHMIED, Meriden, Conn., assignor to the C. F. Monroe Company, Meriden, Conn., a Corporation of Connecticut. Filed Apr. 18, 1902. Serial No. 103,662. Term of patent 3½ years.

Claim.—The design for a cut-glass receptacle as herein shown and described.

277. A copy of a patent record.

Identifying the pattern of a piece of brilliant cut glass in your collection can easily raise the value. More importantly, you experience a wonderful feeling of accomplishment.

Too many times we quit looking and don't explore the many sources easily within our reach. Each step in exploration increases personal knowledge of brilliant cut glass.

PRIMARY SOURCES

When you try to find a pattern name or the source of a piece of cut glass, begin with the most authentic ones.

1. Old Catalogs

Old catalogs provide the most authentic sources for pattern identification. Actually, no one owns a complete set as many threw them away. Some small companies never published catalogs. But everyone can own a few. The American Cut Glass Association has reprinted more than a dozen and have them available for purchase.

2. Patent Records

The application for a patent contained a sketch, the name of the craftsman who created it, and a number along with the assignment to a particular cut glass company. An additional sheet may give more information and name the projected pattern. Unless you go to the United States Patent Office in Washington, D.C., you will not get all of this information. The American Bar Association does have copies of granted patent with a number and name of the company for assignment (277). Having this information may help you locate your pattern.

3. Old Magazine Advertisements

Occasionally, at an estate sale or auction you find copies of old magazines with advertisements that give the pattern and company name of those who produced brilliant cut glass. Companies did advertise in a magazine-type publication sent to stores—jewelry and department—and to mail order houses. One collector found a large number of copies of such publications at an auction. These provided identifications by patterns and companies.

You can rely on these three sources for accurate information on brilliant cut glass. Your next step in identification involves securing clear pictures.

C 279. Compare this photograph of an ice tub (6 D x 4.5 H) with the previous one for clarity.

C 278. A clear picture of an ice tub (6 D x 4.5 H).

PHOTOGRAPHS

The person or group you consult for pattern information needs a sharp picture that shows every detail of the pattern (C 278). You can learn how to arrange different shapes that will not make parts of the pattern fuzzy (C 279). Chapter 12 discusses how to photograph cut glass.

1. Focus

Trust your camera for correct focus. Make sure that you can see the entire pattern. Turn the shape so that the picture will show the linking minor motifs and enough of the major one to recognize it (C 280). In a heavily cut piece you may need to take two pictures. One will show the major motif and the other the linking motif. Often the linking motif actually identifies the pattern. With a floral and geometric pattern, the photograph must show both designs equally (S 281).

If you print your own pictures, you can make the photograph sharper by giving the negative more exposure as seen in (S 282) by comparison to (S 283). When a commercial camera shop prints your picture too light, you can usually return the negative and the photograph for a darker print at a small extra cost. Once you have a clear picture that shows the pattern you will need duplicates.

C 280. The position of the vase (5.5 D x 8 H) shows both the major and minor motifs.

S 281. The photograph must show the geometric and floral motif equally as in the whiskey tumbler (2.5 D x 3 H).

S 282. A whiskey tumbler (2.5 D x 3 H) in Pattern #40 by Dorflinger needs more development.

S 283. The result of more exposure to a negative.

S 284. A photocopy of a picture.　　　　　S 285. A clear picture of a plate (7 D) for photocopying.　　　　　C 286. A photocopy of a plate (6 D) in the Russian Pattern.

2. Duplicates

The company that processed the pictures can make duplicates. A photocopy machine offers a cheaper method of duplication (S 284) from a sharp picture (S 285). With a flat piece, such as a 6-inch plate, you can photocopy the item itself for duplicates (C 286).

Whenever you write for information and whether or not you send a picture, always include a self-addressed, stamped envelop for a reply. Once you have a clear picture of the piece of cut glass, you now contact the different sources that can give you more help on the identification of patterns.

LIBRARIES

At your local library contact the research librarian. Her specialization in research allows her to get answers faster than you ever could. In addition, she can tell you about the available services.

1. Electronic Index

Most libraries no longer use a card index but have an electronic system. You punch in the individual subjects and get the location of the information in the library. The library contains both in and out-of-print books on cut glass. Do check for copies of old catalogs your library may secure on interlibrary loan.

2. Magazines

Most libraries subscribe to two or more antiques magazines, so check several issues at a time for information. These antiques magazine often contain a column by an expert who provides information you need from a picture. When the expert can not secure the information, he or she will print your picture and ask the readers to send in any facts they have. If you want a copy of an article previously printed, you can order a fax at little cost.

Many libraries contain old magazine in storage that often date back to the turn of the century. These contain advertisements for cut glass that name patterns and give addresses of companies. Call the library to find out their viewing schedule. You may find the identification you seek in these. The library can also furnish you with the address and name of museum curators.

MUSEUMS

Museums have grown more interested in American brilliant cut glass. A number have collected old catalogs. So when you are traveling on vacation, try to include a stop at one or more of these museums.

1. Chrysler Museum

This museum displays cut glass with identification cards. When you visit it, take along pictures of pieces you need to identify. Ask to see the curator or assistant so you can show your pictures if you find no matches on display. You may get some quick identifications or facts.

2. Corning Museum

This museum displays cut glass produced by different companies. The research library has microfiche of numerous old catalog you can purchase. Normally, no one can handle the old catalogs, but they will loan you the microfiche and a machine to study cut glass catalogs. Some collectors hesitate to purchase the microfiche as the machine to study it costs too much. Your local library probably owns such a machine and will print copies for more permanent use. The museum also holds annual seminars on glass.

3. Library of Congress

When we checked the card index for the names of old cut glass companies, we found a listing for a Clark catalog. We asked to see it, but the librarian could not locate it. Several weeks later he sent the catalog to our library on loan.

4. Hershey Museum

The curator provided us with information on the museum's famous lamp. This included the size, the number of parts, and various repairs made and initialed. He could not provide a picture as at the time the museum had placed the lamp in storage while doing some renovation. He indicated that the Corning Museum had copies available for sale.

5. Lightner Museum

The curator and his assistant warmly welcomed us. The assistant curator sent us pictures which will appear in this book. Lightner Museum has a very large display of cut glass. Hawkes gave much of this cut glass to Mr. Lightner who established the museum. The collection also includes glass from other companies. This museum owned a late Hawkes catalog they found in the attic after our visit.

6. Smithsonian

This museum owned a Straus catalog which they permitted the American Cut Glass Association to reprint. They displayed a very limited amount of cut glass.

7. Toledo Museum of Art

Interest in Libbey glass dominates this museum. When we asked about library loan of old catalogs, the librarian said the museum owned duplicate copies they loaned to libraries. The museum has since put the catalogs on microfiche which you can purchase. The main display includes the cut glass table in the Neola Pattern and the punch bowl shown at the St. Louis Exposition.

Downstairs across from the research library, you will find a room devoted to identification. The glass cabinets contain different shapes of cut glass with a number. A desk contains a large volume where you locate the index number and learn all the library knows about the piece. From the display and the volume we learned one of our early purchases of cut glass consisted of a souvenir given at the meeting in Toledo of the Daughters of the Nile.

From time to time museums, both national and local, sponsor special exhibits of cut glass. The events publish booklets that contain pictures and information about the displays. The chapters of the American Cut Glass Association may sponsor these exhibits.

AMERICAN CUT GLASS ASSOCIATION

Membership in the American Cut Glass Association can help you learn more about your collection.

1. Catalogs

As previously mentioned a special project of the Association involves the reprinting of old cut glass catalog you can purchase. The Association may combine several catalogs by a company, such as Hawkes or Pairpoint, in one binder. So you have no excuse for not owning old catalogs.

2. Chapters

Belonging to the national Association makes you eligible for membership in the local chapters that meet several times a year. The programs present knowledgeable speakers who personally answer your questions. At most meetings the members bring special pieces of cut glass and give facts about them. In addition, you may bring cut glass and ask for help on identification. A most important advantage consists of meeting collectors and dealers who share your interest.

3. The HOBSTAR

Each month the Association prints a newsletter that contains new information or enlarges on known facts already published in articles. For the matching service you need only submit a picture to receive help from other members to complete a set (C 287). Other times you may need only a tumbler to finish the set (C 288). Another feature asks you to submit a picture for identification (P 289). The members will write and give you any information they know. Dealers provide identification of patterns and sources in their advertisements.

4. National Convention

The Association holds annual conventions in cities across the United States. At the convention you hear knowledgeable speakers, meet dealers who specialize in selling cut glass, and get acquainted with fellow collectors. These contacts provide much information on cut glass. You need only take along your pictures of pieces you hope to identify.

C 287. A set of a bowl (8 D x 4 H) and matching saucers (4.5 D).

C 288. A carafe (5.5 D x 8.5 H) needs a sixth tumbler.

P 289. A vase (6.5 D x 14 H) needed an identification.

PLACES OF INFORMATION

Often you overlook certain places where you can secure information.

1. Bar Association Patent Records

Most Bar Associations have copies of patent records. You can get the location of the Association nearest to you from the office of the state Bar Association. Most locations have copy machines you can use for a nominal charge.

2. Auctions

You have two advantages attending auctions: you meet collectors and dealers. Selling prices depend to a large extent on the members of the audience in competition.

3. Antiques Show and Shops

Here again you meet dealers who have accumulated considerable knowledge on cut glass and enjoy sharing it with you.

PERSONAL CONTACT

Personal contact always offers an opportunity to secure information. Become a good listener. Once a person begins giving you facts, do not interrupt.

1. Dealer

Dealers spend considerable time researching pieces in stock. So whenever you buy a piece of cut glass, ask the dealer for any information. This could include the former owner, the area where the item was purchased, and any other fact. This information may help you in identification of a piece of cut glass. But you need not purchase an item to talk to a dealer.

A few specialize in certain types of information. One dealer at an antiques show mentioned that he liked to do research on signatures. He mentioned general and specific locations of signatures by different companies. "I found a Tuthill signature on the rim of a covered bonbon," he said. That information helped us locate a Tuthill signature on a rim.

2. Fellow Collectors

Most collectors stay alert for any new information on cut glass and enjoy sharing the facts with others. One collector owned a footed nappy exactly like ours, but his contained a Pipkin and Brooks signature. We found the piece in a catalog with the pattern name of Memphis (C 290). As you view collections, always check the signed pieces in case they duplicate your unsigned ones.

3. Glass Repairmen

Skilled artisans who do repair work on cut glass learn to recognize and know patterns. When a collector asked the artisan about a particular piece he repaired, he gave the name and address of the owner. The collector learned the identification from the owner, Pattern #1920, which Sinclaire signed (S 291).

Information surrounds you. You need only reach out and take advantage of the opportunities. By relating bits and pieces, you soon acquire the facts you seek.

C 290. A footed nappy (8 D x 4 H) in Memphis by Pitkin and Brooks identified by a signature on another with the exact pattern.

S 291. A comport (6 D x 4 H) signed Sinclaire in Pattern #1920.

CHAPTER 7 *Previous Identifications*

AMERICAN BRILLIANT CUT GLASS, our first book, published in 1977, identified a number of catalog patterns and pictured pieces with signatures. With very few exceptions our next two books did not repeat these firm identifications. Collectors and dealers continually contact us to purchase this book no longer available.

To assist those who do not have these identifications, this chapter will include a brief statement about the company and add the miter outline, the pattern identification, and the shape. Review the section in Chapter 2 that describes the ten basic miter outlines. We will list the companies in alphabetical order as we did in the original book.

Most cut glass companies named pieces illustrated in the catalogs or magazine advertisements. A few companies identified the pattern with a number under the illustrations. In this book we place "Pattern #_____" before this company figure and "Patent #_____" before a patent number.

AVERBECK CUT GLASS COMPANY
New York City, 1892-1923

Averbeck sold cut glass by mail from its jewelry store. The company published at least one catalog that illustrated cut glass secured from different companies. The catalogs kept the pattern name of the original company, so you will find different patterns with the same name. Averbeck also placed its own signature on pieces.

Geometric Patterns

Border and Miter: Prism, small loving cup (S 292).

Circles: Genoa, whiskey jug (C 293).

Dual Motifs: Boston, 8-inch plate (S 294); Liberty whiskey jug (C 295); Spruce 6-inch plate (S 296).

S 294. A plate (8 D) in Boston Pattern by Averbeck.

S 295. A whiskey jug (8 H) in Liberty Pattern by Averbeck.

S 292. A small loving cup (2.5 D x 3.5 H) in Prism Pattern by Averbeck.

C 293. A whiskey jug (8 H) in Genoa Pattern by Averbeck.

S 296. Averbeck cut this plate (6 D) in Spruce Pattern.

J. D. BERGEN COMPANY
Meriden, Connecticut, 1880-1922

This cutting shop produced some outstanding patterns that appeared in several catalogs. Some pieces contained signatures only.

Geometric Patterns

Miters only: Prism, 8-inch bonbon, (S 297).

Gothic Arch: Dallas, jug, (C 298).

Dual Motif: Elaine, basket, (C 299): Logan, two handled spooner (S 300); Wabash, punch bowl (C 301).

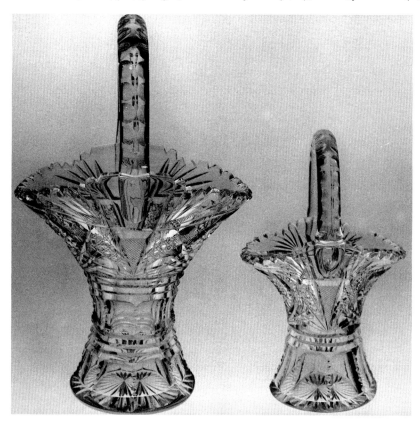

S 297. A bonbon (7 D) in Prism Pattern by Bergen.

C 299. Two sizes of baskets in Elaine Pattern by Bergen.

C 298. Bergen cut this jug (10 H) in Dallas Pattern.

C 300. Bergen cut this spoon holder (5.5 H) in the Logan Pattern.

C 301. Wabash Pattern by Bergen on this punch bowl (12 D x 14 H).

T. B. CLARK AND COMPANY
Honesdale, Pennsylvania, 1884-1930

    Clark established his headquarters in Honesdale as he bought blanks from Christian Dorflinger.

1. Geometric Patterns

Dual Motifs: San Marcos, 6-inch plate (S 302).

2. Signed only

Star: 7-inch plate (S 303).

Gothic Arch: 8-inch bowl (C 304).

Pointed Loops: square dish (S 305).

Dual Motifs: 8-inch bowl (S 306); punch bowl (S 307).

C 304. A bowl (8 D) in a gothic arch outline signed Clark.

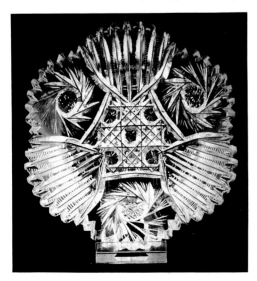

S 302. Clark signed this plate (6 D) in San Marcos Pattern.

S 303. A plate (7 D) signed by Clark in a star outline.

S 305. A pointed loops outline on a square dish signed Clark.

S 306. A bowl (8 D) signed by Clark.

S 307. Clark signed this punch bowl (12 D x 14 H).

C. DORLINGER & SONS
White Mills Pennsylvania, 1852-1921

This factory produced some outstanding pieces of brilliant cut glass. The company supplied both colored and clear blanks to a large number of cutting shops.
Geometric Patterns
Rows: Pattern #80, jug (S 308).
Dual Motifs: Inverness, vase (P 309).

S 308. A jug (5 H) in Pattern #80 by Dorflinger.

P 309. Dorflinger cut this vase (15 H) in the Inverness
Pattern.

O. F. EGGINTON COMPANY
Corning, New York, 1896-1918
O. F. Egginton worked as a manager for Hawkes before he organized his own company.
1. Geometric Pattern
Rows: Calve, tray (P 310).
2. Signed Only
Swirls: 8-inch bowl, (C 311)

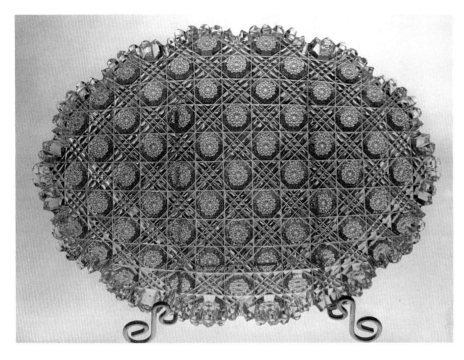

P 310. Egginton designed this pattern originally in Calvé, named for the opera singer Emma Calvé.

C 311. A bowl (8 D) in a swirls outline and signed by Egginton.

H. C. FRY GLASS COMPANY
Rochester, Pennsylvania, 1872-1934
This factory produced some of the finest blanks with a high lead content. Later H. C. Fry introduced the figured blank. Patterns used both simple and ornate designs.
Signed Only
Panels: 20-inch lamp (L 312).
Dual Motifs: 9-inch plate (S 313).

L 312. A lamp (20 H) signed Fry.

S 313. A bowl (9 D) signed by Fry.

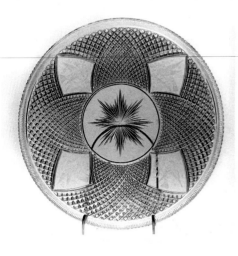

C 314. Cardinal Pattern on a tray (11 D) by Hawkes.

T. G. HAWKES & COMPANY
Corning, New York, 1880-1962

Hawkes came from England to the United States at the urging of J. Hoare. He eventually opened a cutting shop in Corning and bought blanks from Corning Glass Works and later from the Steuben Glass Works.

1. Geometric Pattern
Dual Motifs: Cardinal, 11-inch plate (C 314); Glencoe, 6-inch cologne (C 315).
2. Signed Only
Bars: 11-inch jug with Dominick & Haff Hallmark (C 316); 9-inch square plate (C 317).
Border and Miter: 7-inch oval bowl (S 318).
Gothic Arch: 9-inch square bowl (C 319).
Pointed Loops: 7-in plate (C 320); 7-inch plate (C 321).
Dual Motifs: 9-inch bowl (S 322).
3. Gravic Glass
Three Fruits Pattern, 10-inch bowl (P 323).
Satin Iris, tumbler (S 324).

C 315. Glencoe Pattern on a cologne cut by Hawkes.

C 317. A square dish (9 D) signed Hawkes.

C 316. A jug (11 H) signed by Hawkes with silver hallmark of Dominick and Haff.

C 319. A square bowl (9 D) signed by Hawkes.

S 318. A late pattern in an oval bowl (7 D) signed Hawkes.

C 320. A plate (7 D) with a Hawkes signature.

P 322. A bowl (9 D) with a Hawkes signature.

C 321. A pointed loops outline on a plate (7 D) signed
Hawkes.

P 323. Three Fruits Pattern on a bowl (10 D) in Gravic Glass
and signed by Hawkes.

S 324. A tumbler in Satin Iris Pattern, the last pattern cut by
the Hawkes Company.

S 325. Pattern #5401 with Russian and bars border in an oval tray (10 D) by Hoare.

S 326. A bowl (10 D) in Corncel Pattern by Hoare.

S 327. Hoare called the pattern on this plate (7 D) Nassau.

J. HOARE & COMPANY
Corning, New York, 1853-1920

Hoare worked for Thomas Webb & Sons of England before coming to the United States. He purchased the Brooklyn Flint Glass Company, but in 1868, he moved his cutting shop to Corning. He numbered many of his patterns.

1. Geometric Patterns
Panels: Pattern #5401, 9-inch bowl (S 325).
Dual Motifs: Corncel, 10-inch tray (S 326).
Combination Gothic Arch and Flowers: Nassau 7-inch plate (S 327),
2. Signed Only
Border and Miter: 12-inch vase, (S 328)
Combination Bars and Circles: flower center (C 329).

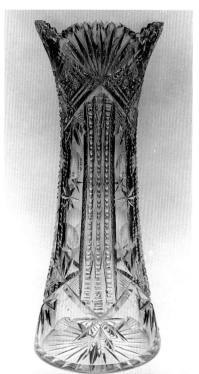

S 328. A vase (12 D) in a border and miter outline and signed Hoare.

C 329. A large flower center signed Hoare.

S 330. A butter tub signed Hobbs Gold Metal.

HOBBS GLASS COMPANY
Wheeling, West Virginia 1845-1891
John L. Hobbs bought the Excelsior Glass Works and later named it Hobbs Glass Company.
Signed Only
Dual Motifs: small butter tub (S 330).

HOPE GLASS WORKS
Providence, Rhode Island 1972-1951
Martin L. Kern organized this company and his son took over in 1891. In 1899, he sold the company to John R. DeGoey.
Signed Only
Star: 8-inch bowl (S 331).
Panels: 9-inch bowl (C 332).

HUNT GLASS COMPANY
Corning, New York 1895-1973
Thomas Hunt and son Harry came to the United States from England in 1880. The company cut some ornate patterns but later used figured blanks.
Signed Only:
Combination Bars and Circles 9-inch bowl (S 333).

S 331. A bowl (8 D) signed by Hope Glass Works.

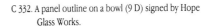

C 332. A panel outline on a bowl (9 D) signed by Hope Glass Works.

S 333. A bowl (9 D) signed by Hunt Glass Company.

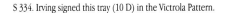

S 334. Irving signed this tray (10 D) in the Victrola Pattern.

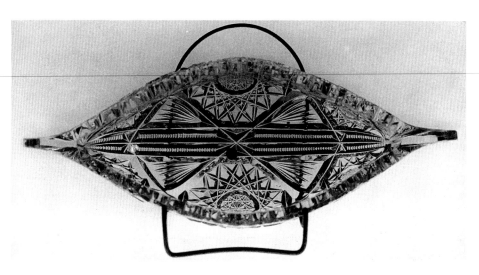

S 335. A relish (9 x 4) in Iowa Pattern signed Irving.

IRVING CUT GLASS COMPANY, INC.
Honesdale, Pennsylvania 1900-1930
This cutting shop worked mostly on figured blanks. It sold to foreign countries in South America, Spain, China, and Japan.
1. Geometric Patterns
Border and Floral: Victrola, 10-inch plate (S 334).
Dual Motifs: Iowa, relish (S 335).
2. Signed Only
Combination Rows and Circles: 8-inch bowl (S 336).

EMIL F. KUPFER, INC.
Brooklyn, New York 1912-1929
Emil F. Kupfer, a cutter, started this company. Patent #44,421, 12-inch tray (S 337).

C 336. A bowl (8 D) with an Irving signature.

S 337. A Patent #44,421 identified this tray by Kupfer.

LIBBEY GLASS COMPANY
Toledo, Ohio 1888-1925

This factory produced a heavy blank for deep and ornate cutting. The company early led in the production of ornate patterns and of using signatures.

1. Geometric Pattern

Bars: Kingston, 10-inch tray (C 338).

Rows: Glenda, 9-inch bowl (C 339).

Swirls: Star and Feather, 8-inch bowl (C 340).

Pointed Loops: Delphos, 10-plate (C 341).

Dual Motifs: Jewel, stemware (C 342); Princess, ice bowl (C 343); Rajah, covered butter and plate (C 344).

Combination border and dual motifs: Silver Thread, 4.5-inch jug (C 345).

2. Signed Only

Rows: 12-inch vase (C 346); 8-inch plate (S 347).

Panels: 12-inch vase (C 348).

Dual Motifs: 8-inch bowl (C 349); 10.5-inch plate (C 350); 12-inch decanter (C 351); 3.5 footed salt (S 352).

3. Patent Record

Combination of pointed loops and circles: Patent #38,001 bonbon (C 353).

4. Floral Pattern

Swirl: Morgan, 8-inch bowl (S 354).

Dual Motifs: Libbey, 12-inch tray (C 355)

C 339. Libbey named the pattern on this bowl (9 D) Glenda.

C 338. Libbey cut a bars outline on this tray (10 D) in the Kingston Pattern.

C 340. Libbey named this bowl (8 D) with a swirls outline the Star and Feather pattern.

C 341. This plate (10 D) Libbey called Delphos Pattern.   C 342. A set of stemware in Jewel Pattern by Libbey.

C 343. An ice bowl in Princess Pattern signed Libbey.

C 344. A covered butter and plate in Rajah Pattern signed Libbey.

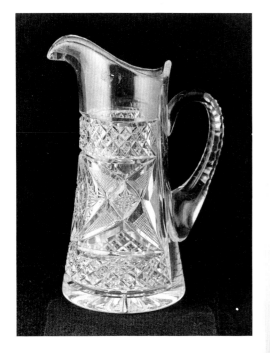

C 345. Libbey called this pattern on a jug (4.5 H) Silver Thread.

C 346. A vase (12 H) signed Libbey.

S 347. A plate (8 D) signed Libbey.

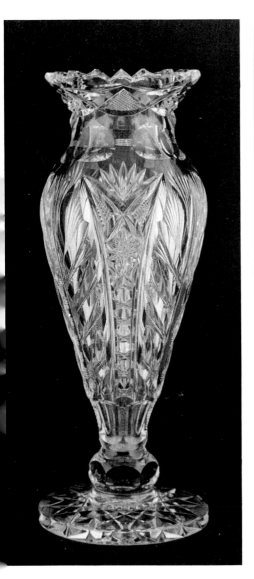

C 348. A vase (12 H) in a panel outline signed by Libbey.

C 349. A bowl (8 D) signed by Libbey.

C 350. A tray (10.5 D) with a Libbey signature.

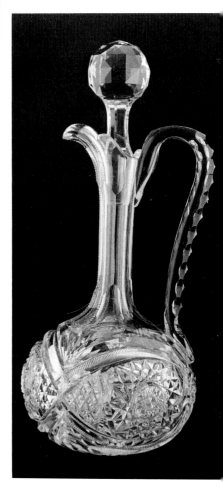

C 351. Libbey signed this decanter (12 H).

S 352. A footed salt (3.5 H) signed by Libbey.

C 353. Patent #38,001 identified this bonbon by Libbey.

S 354. A bowl (8 D) with a floral border shows the Morgan Pattern by Libbey.

C 355. Libbey called the design on this tray (12 D) the Libbey Pattern.

MAPLE CITY GLASS COMPANY
Hawley, Pennsylvania 1900-1911

J. S. O'Connor who owned this company published ten catalogs. T. B. Clark eventually purchased the company.

Geometric Pattern
Rows: Devonshire, 10-inch flower holder (C 356).
Pointed Loops: Lista, 10-inch plate (C 357).
Dual Motifs: Weldon, 4-inch individual olive (S 358).

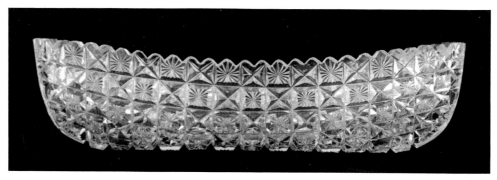

C 356. A flower holder (10 x 4) in Devonshire Pattern and signed by Maple City.

C 357. A tray (10 D) in Lista Pattern by Maple City.

S 358. An individual olive in Weldon Pattern by Maple City.

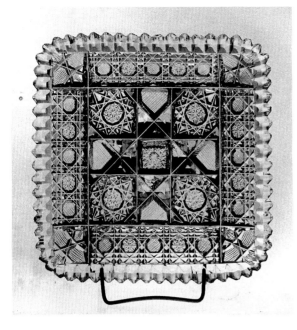

C 359. Meridan gave this square plate (7 D) the identification of Pattern #227F.

C 360. A cheese dome and plate in Plymouth Pattern by Meridan.

MERIDEN CUT GLASS COMPANY
Meriden Connecticut 1895-1923

The Meriden Silver Plate Company organized the Meriden Cut Glass Company to cut glass for silver appointments. In 1898, both became a part of International Silver Company.
Geometric Pattern
Bars: 227F, 7-inch square plate (C 359).
Dual Motifs: Plymouth, covered cheese and plate (C 360).

JOHN S. O'CONNOR
Hawley, Pennsylvania 1890-1910

O'Connor who formerly worked for Dorflinger opened this factory.
Geometric Pattern
Rows: Princess, 10-inch bowl (S 361).

OHIO CUT GLASS COMPANY
Bowling Green, Ohio 1904-1912

This company operated a cutting shop for Pitkin and Brooks. Thomas Singleton managed the shop and designed the patterns.
Patent #36,866, bonbon (C 362).

PAIRPOINT CORPORATION
New Bedford, Massachusetts 1880-1938

Mt. Washington Glass Works organized this company as a subsidiary to add silver appointment to cut glass. Eventually the subsidiary took over the parent firm and became the Pairpoint Corporation.
Geometric Pattern
Dual Motifs: Avilla, 10-inch tall comport (C 363).

S 361. The Princess Pattern on a bowl (10 D) cut by John S. O'Connor.

C 362. A bonbon in Patent #36,866 assigned to Ohio Cut Glass Company.

C 363. A comport (10 H) in the Avilla Pattern by Pairpoint.

S 364. Pitkin and Brooks named the pattern on this comport (7 H) Border.

PITKIN & BROOKS
Chicago, Illinois C 1872-1930

Edward H. Pitkin and Jonathan W. Brooks owned this factory. It ranked as one of the largest distributors of glassware and crockery in the Mid-West.

1. Geometric Pattern

Border and Miter: Border, 7-inch comport (S 364).

Pointed Loops: Plymouth, 8-inch bowl (C 365).

Dual Motifs: Belmont, 8-inch bowl (C 366); Cleo,

8-inch bowl (S 367); Myrtle, 10-inch tray (S 368); Rajah, sugar and cream (S 369).

2. Signed Only

Border and Miter: 12-inch celery (S 370).

C 365. A bowl (8 D) by Pitkins and Brooks in the Plymouth Pattern.

C 366. Pitkin and Brooks named the pattern on this bowl (8 D) Belmont.

S 367. The Cleo Pattern Pitkin and Brooks cut on this bowl (8 D).

S 368. A tray (10 D) in Myrtle Pattern by Pitkin and Brooks.

S 369. A sugar and cream set by Pitkin and Brooks in the Rajah Pattern.

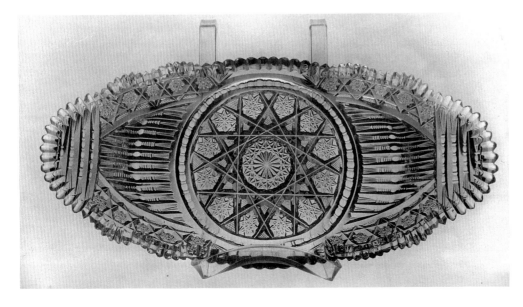

S 370. A celery (12) signed by Pitkin and Brooks.

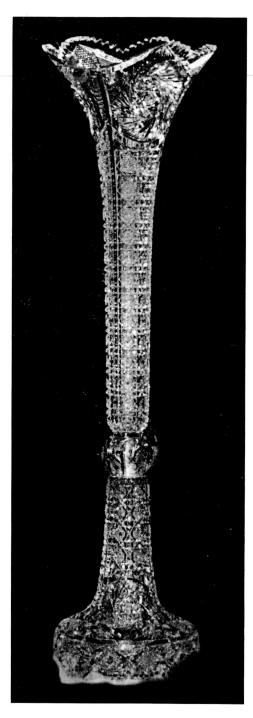

P 371. A three-part vase in Empress Pattern by Quaker City.

QUAKER CITY CUT GLASS COMPANY
Philadelphia, Pennsylvania 1902-1927
    This cutting shop produced very ornate patterns and increased the descriptions in the catalogs.
Geometric Pattern
Combination Rows and Borders: Empress, 20-inch three piece vase (P 371).

H. P. SINCLAIRE & COMPANY
Corning, New York 1904-1928
    H. P. Sinclaire, a former partner of Hawkes, organized the company and served as the designer. As a naturalist he created designs from nature in copper wheel engraving.
1. Geometric Pattern
Dual Motifs: Baronial, flower center (S 372).
Combination Border and Panel: Queens, 10-inch bowl (C 373).
2. Signed Only
Gothic Arch: 8-inch bowl (C 374); 9-inch bowl (S 375).

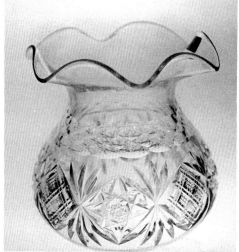

S 372. A flower center in Baronial Pattern by Sinclaire.

C 374. A bowl (8 D) signed Sinclaire.

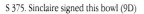

S 375. Sinclaire signed this bowl (9D)

C 373. A bowl (10 D) Sinclaire named Queens Pattern.

S 377. A jug (9 H) signed by Straus.

S 376. A carafe signed by Straus.

S 379. A nappy (6 D) signed by Tuthill.

S 378. Straus signed this bowl (8 D).

L. STRAUS & SONS
New York City, 1888

Lazarus Straus came from Bavaria and worked as a salesman for a china and glassware import company. In 1888, he organized his own firm and began cutting glass.
Signed Only
Dual Motifs: carafe (S 376); 9-inch tall jug (S 377); low 10-inch bowl (C 378).

TUTHILLL CUT GLASS COMPANY,
Middletown, New York 1894-1923

Charles G. Tuthill with James and Susan Tuthill organized this company. Charles, the designer, became famous for his intaglio patterns.
1. Signed Only
Bars: 6-inch nappy (S 379); 10-inch tall comport (C 380).
Dual Motifs: 6-inch plate (C 381); 8 x 6 bonbon (C 382); 6-inch saucer (S 383); mayonnaise set (C 384); 9-inch bowl (S 385); 15-inch tall basket (C 386); 7-inch plate (S 387).
2. Geometric and Intaglio
Intaglio grape and border: Grape (C 388).

C 380. Tuthill signed this comport (6 x 10).

C 381. A plate (6 D) signed by Tuthill.

C 382. Tuthill signed this bonbon (8 x 6).

C 383. A saucer (6 D) with a Tuthill signature.

C 384. A mayonnaise set identified by a Tuthill signature.

S 385. A bowl (9 D) signed by Tuthill.

S 387. A plate (7 D) signed Tuthill.

C 386. A basket (15 H) has a Tuthill signature.

C 388. A tray (15 D) called Grape Pattern in Tuthill's intaglio with geometric border.

UNION GLASS COMPANY
Somerville, Massachusetts 1851-1927

Union Glass Company specialized in cut glass blanks but later produced figured blanks. The company issued several large catalogs illustrating the shapes of the blanks recommended for tableware. No record verifies when Union turned to making liners which give some pieces of cut glass identification.
Signed on Liner
Pointed Loops: jardiniere (C 389).
Dual Motifs: 7-inch fern (S 390); tall jardiniere (C 391).

C 389. A jardiniere with a liner signed Union Cut Glass Company.

S 390. A fern (7 D) with a Union liner.

C 391. Heavily cut jardiniere has a Union liner.

S 392. A Van Heusen signature appears on this plate (7 D).

VAN HEUSEN CHARLES
Albany, New York 1893-1943

This company served as an agent for Libbey and other glass companies.
Signed Only
Star: 7-inch plate (S 392).

WILCOX SILVER PLATE COMPANY
New York

Supposedly this company worked with Meriden Silver Plate Company in adding silver to cut glass. Along with others, this company merged with International Silver.
Signed on Silver
Star: 6 D x 7 H comport (S 393).
Dual Motifs: 9-inch bitters bottle (S 394).

S 393. This comport has a Wilcox hallmark on the silver.

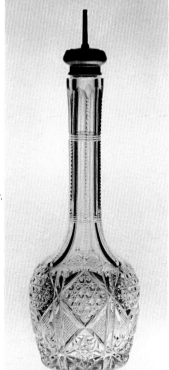

S 394. A bitters bottle with the Wilcox hallmark on the silver.

S 395. A sugar and cream signed Wright.

S 396. A floral pattern on a sugar and cream signed Wright.

WRIGHT RICH CUT GLASS
Anderson, Indiana 1904-1915
George W. Wright and Thomas W. Wright operated this cutting shop.
1. Geometric Pattern
Dual Motifs: sugar and cream (S 395).
2. Floral: sugar and cream (S 396).

CANADIAN CUT GLASS COMPANIES

These companies bought blanks from factories in the United States as well as from Europe. Signatures frequently contained both that of the producer and the agent. These four companies represent the largest one, but a number of smaller companies did produce cut glass.

1. Gowans, Kent & Company Limited
Signed. Dual Motifs: 5-inch bowl (S 397).
2. Gundy-Clapperton Company
Geometric Pattern
Panel: Coronation, 8-inch bowl (C 398).
Signed Only
Border and Flower, bonbon (S 399).
Panels: 12-inch tall jug (C 400).
Dual Motifs: 8-inch bowl (S 401).
3. Lakefield Cut Glass Company
Geometric and Floral. Dual Motifs: Lakefield, 10-inch comport (S 402).
4. Roden Brothers
1. Geometric

S 397. Gowans, Kent of Canada signed this bowl (5 D).

C 398. The Coronation pattern on this bowl (9 D) has a Gundy-Clapperton signature.

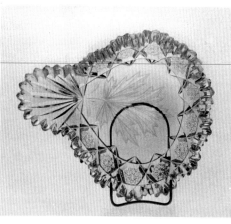

S 399. This bonbon has two signatures: Gundy-Clapperton and that of Agent Dingwall.

C 400. A jug (12 H) signed by Gundy-Clapperton.

S 401. A bowl (8 D) with the Gundy-Clapperton signature.

S 402. A comport (7 D x 10 H) in Lakefield Pattern by the Lakefield Company.

Dual Motifs: 10-inch tall comport (C 403).
2. Signed Only
Floral: cream and sugar (S 404).

This concludes the identifications by patterns or by signatures from AMERICAN BRILLIANT CUT GLASS. May you identify some of the cut glass in your collection with the help of this information.

C 403. A large comport signed by Roden Brothers.

C 404. A cream in a floral pattern signed by Roden Brothers.

CHAPTER 8 *New Identifications of Patterns*

Knowledge adds excitement to collecting American brilliant cut glass. Nothing compares to your elation when you discover the pattern or source of cut glass pieces in your collection. May this new information on patterns and signatures help you identify the still "unknowns" in your collection.

ALMY & THOMAS
Cutting Shop
Bars: signed, nappy (S 405).

ALLEN CUT GLASS COMPANY
Cutting Shop
Dual Motifs: Dupont, bonbon (C 406).
Floral: Lotus, bowl (S 407).

S 405. A nappy (6 D) signed by Almy and Thomas.

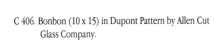

C 406. Bonbon (10 x 15) in Dupont Pattern by Allen Cut
Glass Company.

S 407. Bonbon (6 D) in Lotus Pattern by Allen.

C 408. Dresser tray (10 x 5), Patent #27,062 by American
Cut Glass Company.

C 409. Bowl (8 D), Patent #27,061 by American Cut Glass
Company.

P 410. A tray (12 D) in Patent #27,060 by American Cut
Glass Company.

AMERICAN CUT GLASS COMPANY
Cutting Shop
Border and Miter: Patent #27,062, tray (C 408).
Star: Patent #27,061, bowl (C 409).
Combination Star and Gothic Arch: Patent #27,060, tray (P 410).

S 411. A bowl (7 D) in Acme Pattern by Averbeck.

S 412. Averbeck signed this relish (7 x 3.5) in Canton Pattern.

M. J. AVERBECK MANUFACTURER
Cutting Shop and Jewelry
Dual Motifs: Acme, bowl (S 411); Canton, relish (S 412); Naples, vase (P 413); Vienna, tray (C 114).

P 413 A vase (12 H) in Naples Pattern by Averbeck.

C 414. A tray (14 x 7.5) by Averbeck in the Vienna Pattern.

J. D. BERGEN COMPANY
Cutting Shop

1. Geometric Pattern
Miter and Border: Ivy, jug (C 415).
Gothic Arch: Excelsior, jug (P 416).
Dual Motifs: Cassia, toothpick (S 417); **Dora**, covered comport (P 418); **Globe**, bowl (S 419); **Renwich**, decanter (P 420); **Sheldon**, vase (C 421); **Tyroee**, flower center (P 422); **Viceroy**, horseradish bottle, (C 423).

S 417. Cassia Pattern on this toothpick holder (3.5 H) by Bergen.

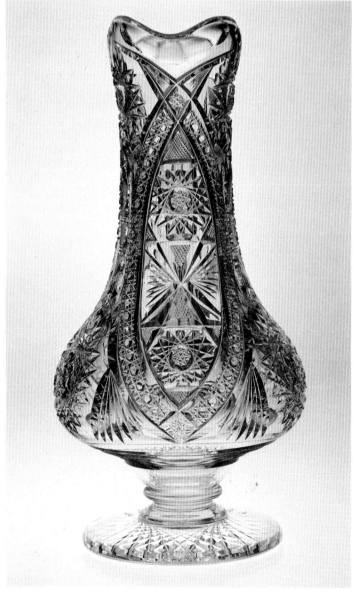

C 415. Bergen name the pattern on this jug (8.5 H) Ivy.

P 416. A footed jug (18 D x 12 H) in the Excelsior Pattern by Bergen.

P 418. A covered comport (13 H) in the Dora Pattern by Bergen.

S 419. Bergen called this pattern on a bowl (8 D) Globe.

C 421. A vase (12 H) in Sheldon Pattern by Bergen.

P 420. A decanter (12 H) in the Renwich Pattern by Bergen.

P 422. The Tyroee Pattern by Bergen on a flower center.

C 423. Viceroy Pattern on a horseradish jar (2.5 D x 5.5 H) by Bergen.

S 424. A nappy (5 D) signed Bergen with the two worlds signature.

S 427. Bergen patented the pattern on this bowl (9 D) September 22, 1891.

S 425. A cologne (4 D x 6 H) in Aster Pattern by Bergen.

2. Floral
Horseshoe and Flower, signed with two worlds signature, nappy (S 424);
Aster, cologne (S 425).

3. Patent
Rows: #23,317, bowl (S 426);
Swirls: Patented September, 22, 1891, bowl (P 427)

BLACKMER CUT GLASS COMPANY
Cutting Shop

Geometric Patterns
Rows: Celtic, comport (C 428); Medina, comport (P 429); Sultana, flower center (C 430).
Border and Miter: Pattern #16, decanter, (C 431).
Star: Estelle, bowl (S 432).
Panels: Nordel, vase (P 433).
Pointed Loops: Corona, small plate (C 434).
Dual Miters: Eudora, sugar and cream (S 435); Iola, two-handled nappy (S 436); Marlo, bonbon (S 437); Oregon, jug (C 438); Richmond, vase (C 439); Triton, bonbon (C 440)..

S 426. Bergen received Patent #23,317 for design on this bowl (9 D).

C 428. A comport (9 D x 6.5 H) in Celtic Pattern by Blackmer.

P 429. The Medina Pattern by Blackmer on a comport (9 D x 9.5 H).

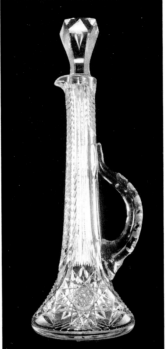

C 431. Pattern #16 by Blackmer on a decanter.

S 432. The Estelle Pattern on a bowl (9 D) by Blackmer.

C 430. A flower center (12 D x 11 H) in the Sultana Pattern by Blackmer.

P 433. A vase (7.5 D x 11 H) in Nordel Pattern by Blackmer.

C 434. Corona Pattern on a plate (6 D) by Blackmer.

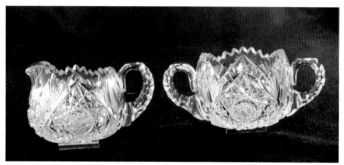

S 435. A sugar and cream in Eudora Pattern by Blackmer.

C 438. A jug (10 H) in Oregon Pattern by Blackmer.

S 436. A two-handled nappy (6 D) in Iola Pattern by Blackmer.

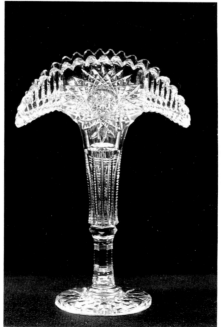

C 440. A bonbon by Blackmer in the Triton Pattern.

S 437. The Marlo Pattern on this bonbon (6 D) by Blackmer.

C 439. A vase (9 H) by Blackmer in the Richmond Pattern.

T. B. CLARK AND COMPANY
Cutting shop

1. Geometric Pattern
Bars: Newport, decanter (C 441).
Rows: Jewel, bell (C 442).
Border and Miter: Anemone, vase (C 443); Stratford, vase (C 444).
Gothic Arch: Desdemona, small plate (S 445); Pontiac, bowl (C 446).
Panels: American Beauty, vase (C 447); Flute, decanter (S 448); Ionian, tray (P 449).
Swirls: Marbella, comport (S 450).
Circles: El Tova, footed bowl (P 451).
Dual Motifs: Adonis, celery (C 452); Canna, vase (C 453); Carot, bowl (C 454); Florentine, creamer (S 455); Harvest, celery (S 456); Reaper, flower bowl (S 457); Winola, decanter (C 458).

C 443. A vase (10 H) in Anemone Pattern by Clark.

C 444. Stratford Pattern by Clark on a vase (10 H).

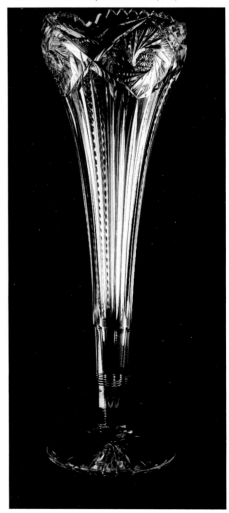

C 441. Newport Pattern by Clark on a decanter (12 H).

C 442. A bell in Jewel Pattern by Clark.

S 445. Desdemona Pattern by Clark on a plate (7 D).

C 446. Pontiac Pattern by Clark on a bowl (8 D).

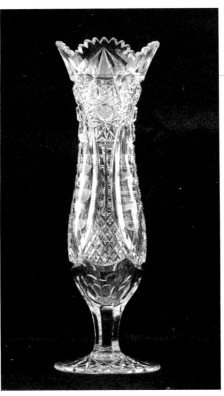

C 447. American Beauty Pattern by Clark on vase (13 H).

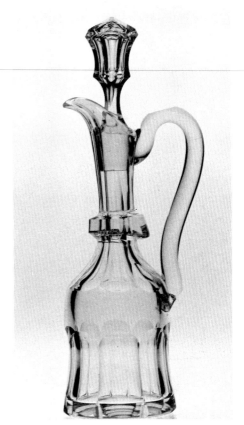

S 448. A decanter (10 H) in Flute Pattern by Clark.

2. Signed Only
Bars: jug (P 459).
Pointed Loops: tray (P 460); small plate (C 461).
Dual Motifs: celery (S 462); celery (S 463); square dish (C 464); whiskey bottle (C 465).

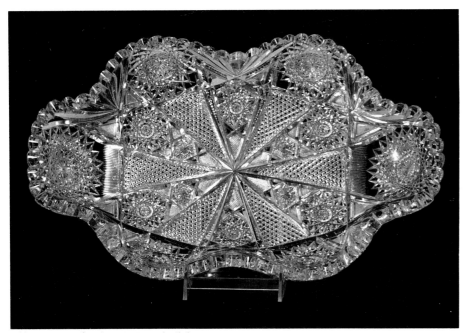

P 449. A tray (8.5 x 16) in the Ionian Pattern by Clark.

S 450. A comport (5.5 D x 6 H) in the Marbella Pattern by Clark.

C 453. The Canna Pattern by Clark on a vase (20 H).

P 451. The El Tova Pattern on a footed bowl (8.5 D x 9 H) by Clark.

C 454. A bowl (9 D) in the Carot Pattern by Clark.

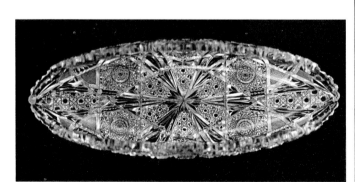

C 452. A celery (12) in the Adonis Pattern by Clark.

C 455. A cream to a set in Florentine Pattern by Clark.

S 456. A celery (10) in Clark's Harvest Pattern.

S 457. A flower holder (12.5) in Reaper Pattern by Clark.

C 458. The Winola Pattern by Clark on matching decanters (12 H).

P 459. A tanker jug (12 H) signed Clark.

P 460. A tray (11.5 D) signed Clark.

S 463. A celery (11.5 x 6) signed Clark.

C 461. A plate (6 D) signed Clark.

S 462. A celery (12 x 8) signed Clark.

C 464. A square dish (8 D) by Clark.

C 465. A whiskey bottle (13 H) with a Clark signature.

C 466. A jug (7.5 H) in Belmont Pattern by Dorflinger.

C 468. A cologne in Pattern #682 by Dorflinger.

S 467. Pattern #210 on matching cordial jug by Dorflinger.

C. DORLINGER AND SONS
Factory

Geometric Pattern
Rows: Belmont, jug (C 466); Pattern #210, cordials jugs (S 467); Pattern #682 cologne (C 468).
Panels: Engadine, vase (C 469).
Dual Motifs: mayonnaise set (C 470); Old Colony, tumbler & jug (C 471); candlestick (C 472).

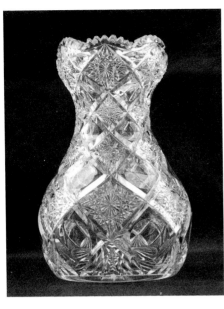

C 469. A vase (10.5 H) in
Engadine by
Dorflinger

C 471.2. A jug (9 H) in Old
Colony Pattern by
Dorflinger.

S 470. A mayonnaise set with a
matt background by
Dorflinger.

C 471.1. A tumbler in Old
Colony Pattern by
Dorflinger.

C 472. Candlestick by
Dorflinger.

S 473. Whiskey decanter (4.5 D x 7 H) in Berkshire Pattern signed Egginton.

O. F. Egginton Company
Cutting Shop

Geometric Pattern
Rows: Berkshire, whiskey decanter (S 473).
Star: Carnival, bowl (C 474).
Panels: Iroquois, vase (C 475).
Pointed Loops: Roman, plate (C 476).

C 475. A vase (12 H) in Iroquois Pattern by Egginton.

C 476. A tray (14 D) in Roman Pattern by Egginton.

C 474. Bowl (8 D) in Carnival Pattern signed Egginton.

EMPIRE CUT GLASS COMPANY
Cutting shop

Geometric Pattern
Bars: Madame, two handled nappy (C 477),
Panels: Viola, vase (C 478).
Dual Motifs: Albert, goblet (C 479); Renton, dresser set (C 480).
Combination Bars and Dual Motifs: Plaza, celery (C 481).

C 479. A goblet (5.5 H) in Albert
Pattern by Empire.

C 477. A two-handled nappy (8 D) in Madame Pattern by Empire.

C 478. The Viola Pattern on a vase (12 H) by Empire.

C 480. A dresser set in
Renton Pattern by
Empire.

C 481. A celery (5.5 x 13) in Plaza Pattern by Empire.

S 482. Napkin rings in Prism by Bergen (left) and Pattern #1 by Elmira (right).

ELMIRA CUT GLASS COMPANY
Cutting Shop

Geometric Pattern
Dual Motifs: Pattern #1, napkin ring (S 482); Pattern #21 upright spooner (C 483); Pattern #39, spoon tray (S 484).

C 483. A spooner (4.5 D x 5.5 H) in Pattern #21 by Elmira.

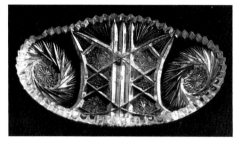

S 484. A spoon tray (7.5 x 4.5) in Pattern #39 by Elmira.

H. C. Fry Glass Company
Factory

1. Geometric Pattern
Bars: Carnation, bowl (S 485); Elba, bread tray (C 486); Keystone, bowl (C 487).
Border and Floral: Asteroid, sandwich tray (S 488).
Star: Nashville, bowl (S 489).
Pointed Loops: Spokane, spooner (S 490).
Dual Motifs: Alexis, comport (S 491); American, hexagon bowl (C 492); Freedom, flower center (C 493); Heart, tumbler (S 494); ' Sunburst, bowl (S 495).

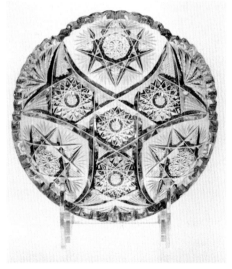

S 485. A bowl (9 D) in Carnation Pattern by Fry.

C 486. A bread tray (12 x 8) signed Fry in Elba Pattern.

C 487. The Keystone Pattern by Fry on a bowl (10 D).

S 488. Sandwich tray (10 D) in Asteroid Pattern by Fry.

S 489. A bowl (8 D) in Nashville Pattern by Fry.

C 492. Hexagon bowl (6 D) on peg feet in American Pattern by Fry.

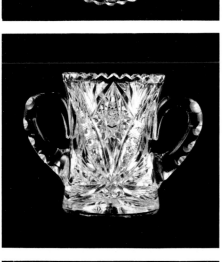

S 490. A spooner (3.5 D x 4.5 H) in Spokane Pattern by Fry.

C 493. Freedom Pattern by Fry on a flower center (5.5 x 9 H).

S 491. Alexis Pattern by Fry on a comport (5.5 C x 3.5 H).

S 494. Heart Pattern by Fry on a whiskey tumbler (3 D x 3.5 H).

S 495. Sunburst Pattern by Fry on a bowl (8 D).

C 496. A bowl (8 D) signed Fry.

C 497. A bowl (9.5 D) signed Fry.

2. Signed Only
Dual Motifs: bowl (S 496); bowl (C 49~ ').

T. J. HAWKES AND Company
Cutting Shop

1. Geometric Pattern
Bars: Patent #19,865, tray (S 498).
Rows: Crete, bonbon (S 499); Devonshire, nappy (S 500); Harmony, dresser set (P 501); Juno, tumbler (S 502); Norwood, tray (S 503); Table Diamond, two decanters (P 504).
Border and Punte: Flute and Greek Key, cigarette jar (S 505).
Panels: Minerva, bowl (S 506); Mona, bowl (C 507); Pattern #1422, bonbon (C 508).
Dual Motifs: Argo, glove box (C 509); Delhi, oil (C 510); Elba, bonbon (S 511); Jersey, candlestick (C 512); Oxford, cologne (S 513); Pilgram, mayonnaise (S 514); Pattern #2, butter pat (S 515); Pattern #3, bowl (S 516).

S 498. A tray (10 D) Patent #19,865 by Hawkes.

S 499. A bonbon (7 D) in Crete Pattern by Hawkes.

S 500. A handled nappy (5.5 D) in the first Devonshire Pattern by Hawkes.

S 503. Plate (10 D) in Norwood by Hawkes.

P 501. Footed puff box and hair receiver in Harmony Pattern by Hawkes.

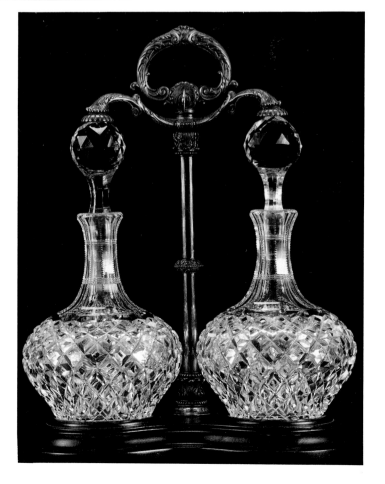

P 504. Table Diamond Pattern on two decanters signed Hawkes.

S 502. A tumbler in Juno Pattern signed Hawkes.

S 505. Cigarette jar (7 H) in Flutes and Greek Key Pattern by Hawkes.

S 506. A bowl (6 D) in Minerva Pattern by Hawkes.

C 507. The Mona Pattern by Hawkes adorns this bowl (8 D).

C 508. Pattern #1422 identifies this bonbon (7 D) by Hawkes.

C 509. Argo Pattern by Hawkes on this glove box (6.5 x 3 x 3.5 H).

C 510. An oil (7 H) in Delhi Pattern by Hawkes.

C 511. A heart bonbon (4 D) in Elba Pattern by Hawkes.

S 514. The Pilgrim Pattern by Hawkes on a mayonnaise bowl (5 D).

C 512. Candleholder (5.5 D) in Jersey Pattern by Hawkes.

S 515. Hawkes numbered this Pattern #2 on a butter pat.

S 516. A bowl (9 D) in Pattern #3 by Hawkes.

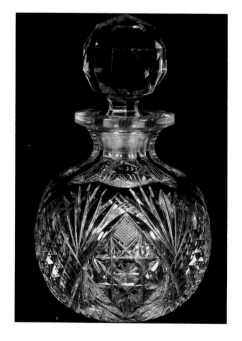

S 513. A cologne in Oxford Pattern by Hawkes.

S 517. A comport (9 H) signed Hawkes.

2. Signed only
Rows: comport (S 517); whiskey jug (C 518); Rose globe (C 519).
Border and Miter: bitters bottle (C 520); candlesticks (C 521).
Star: tray (C 522); jug (C 523).
Panels: jug (C 524); crimped bowl (P 525); crimped bowl (P 526); crimped bowl (P 527).
Pointed Loops: square bowl (S 528); square bowl (S 529),
Circles: punch cup (S 530); tray (L 531).
Dual Motifs: catsup bottle (S 532); pair of candlesticks (C 533); tray (P 534); basket: (P 535).
Combination Pointed Loops and Circles: bread tray (P 536).

C 519. A rose globe (5.5 D x 5 H) with a Hawkes signature.

S 518. A whiskey jug (4.5 D x 8.5 H) signed Hawkes.

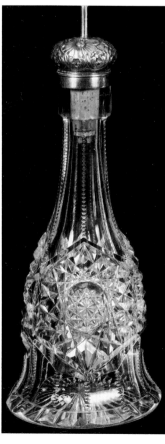

C 520. A bitters bottle (8 H) signed Hawkes.

C 521. A pair of candlesticks signed Hawkes.

C 524. Hawkes signed this jug (8 H).

C 522. Hawkes signed this tray (14.5 D).

C 523. A jug (5.5 D x 8 H) signed Hawkes.

P 525. A bowl (10 D) with crimped rim signed Hawkes.

P 526. A crimped bowl (10 D) signed Hawkes.

S 529. A square dish (9 D) similar to S 528 signed Hawkes.

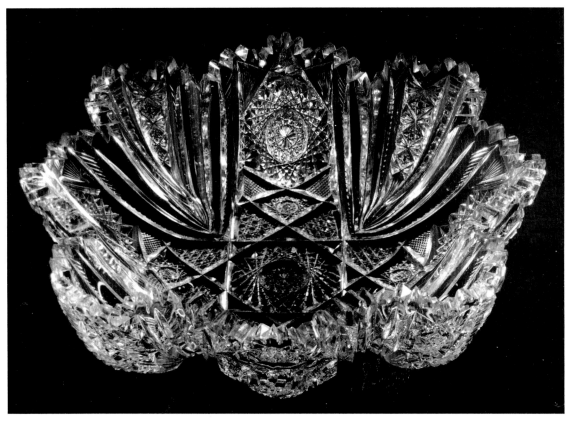

P 527. Hawkes signed this crimped bowl (10.5 D x 8 H).

S 528. A square dish (9 D) signed Hawkes.

S 530. A punch cup signed Hawkes.

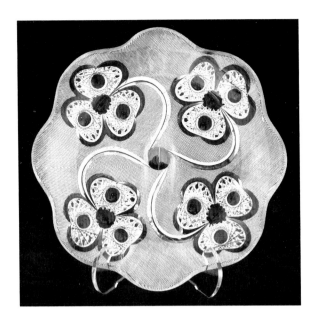

L 531. Hearts form petals on the flowers of this tray (13 D) with a matt background signed Hawkes.

S 532. A catsup bottle (6 H) signed Hawkes.

P 534. Hawkes signed this tray (14 D).

P 535. A basket (8 D x 4 H) signed Hawkes.

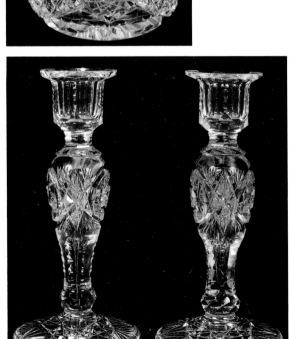

C 533. A pair of candlesticks (8 H) signed Hawkes.

P 536. Hawkes signed this oval bread tray (10.5 x 7.5) on a miter.

3. Geometrics and Engraving
Rows: Strawberry-Diamond and floral squares, jug (S 537); pointed diamond and floral medallions, jug (S 538).
Border and Scene: Pheasant, plate (C 539).
Gothic Arch: plate (C 540).
Floral: car vase (S 541); Graphic Cosmos, (5 542).

S 537. Clear diamonds frame birds, flowers, and berries on this jug (10.5 H) signed Hawkes.

S 538. Hawkes used medallions for flowers on this whiskey jug (8.5 H).

C 539. Hawkes combined flowers with gothic arches on this plate (9 D).

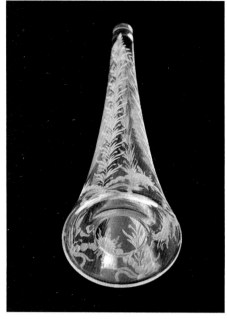

S 541. A car vase (8 H) signed Hawkes.

C 540. Hawkes called this engraved plate (5 D) Pheasant and signed it.

S 542. A flower holder (9 D) signed Hawkes in Graphic Cosmo Pattern.

GEORGE H. HIBBLER AND COMPANY
Cutting Shop

Geometric Pattern
Gothic Arch: Patent #22,663, bowl (S 543).

S 543. A bowl (8 D) by George H. Hibbler in Patent #22,663.

J. HOARE AND COMPANY
Cutting Shop

1. Geometric Pattern
Rows: Harvard, vase (P 544): name unreadable in Hoare catalog, decanter (S 545).
Border and Miter: Prism, vase (C 546); **Tasso**, Worcestershire bottle (S 547).
Dual Motifs: Cairo, decanter (S 548); **Crystal City**, cologne (P 549); **Eleanor** with 8-point star added, tray (C 550); **Monarch**, ice bowl with stopper handles (C 551); **Naples**, decanter (C 552); **Sparkler**, nappy (S 553); **York**, comport (S 554); **Yucatan**, celery (C 555).

C 546. A vase (9 H) in Prism Pattern by Hoare.

P. 544. A vase (24 H) in Harvard Pattern signed Hoare.

S 545. A decanter pictured in the Hoare catalog but the name not legible.

S 547. A Worcestershire bottle in Tasso Pattern by Hoare.

S 548. An oil in Cairo Pattern by Hoare.

P 549. A version of Crystal City Pattern on this cologne.

C 550. Hoare added 8-point stars to the Eleanor Pattern on this tray (10.25 x 9.5).

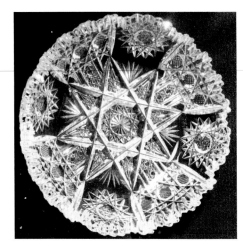

S 553. A nappy (6 D) in Sparkler Pattern by Hoare.

C 551. Faceted stoppers formed the handles on this ice bowl (9.5 D x 5 H) in Monarch Pattern by Hoare.

S 554. A comport (8 H) in York Pattern by Hoare.

S 555. A Hoare celery (13 x 4.5) in Yucata Pattern.

C 552. Hoare cut a matching stopper on this decanter in Naples Pattern.

2. Numbered Pattern
Bars: Pattern #8677, olive dish (S 556).
Rows: Pattern #1554 and Harvard, napkin rings (S 557).
Swirls: Pattern #1531, ink bottle (C 558).
Dual Motifs: Pattern #9546, vase (C 559); Pattern #9595, fruit bowl (C 560): Pattern #9922, sauce dish (S 561).

C 558. Pattern #1531 on an ink bottle (4.4 H) by Hoare.

S 556. Pattern #8677 by Hoare in an olive dish.

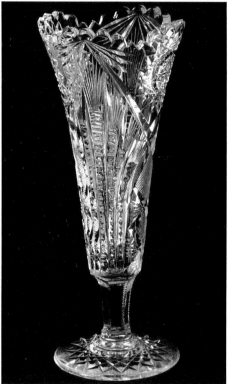

C 559. A vase (10 H) in #9546 Pattern by Hoare.

S 561. A mayonnaise in Pattern #9922 by Hoare.

S 557. Two napkin rings by Hoare, Pattern #1554 (left) and Harvard Pattern (right).

C 560, A fruit bowl (13.5 D) in Pattern #9595 by Hoare.

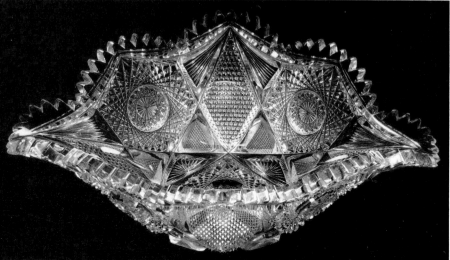

C 565. A tray (14 x 8) signed Hoare.

C 562. A decanter (15.5 H) in St. Louis Diamond signed Hoare.

3. Signed Only

Rows: decanter (C 562).
Border and Miter: tray (P 563).
Panels: mayonnaise bowl (C 564); tray (C 565); tumbler (S 566).
Swirls: vase (C 567); comport (C 568).
Dual Motifs: butter pat (S 569); individual salt (S 570); vase (C 571); jug (C 572); comport (S 573); bowl (C 574); decanter (P 575); square bowl (C 576); bowl (C 577); oval bowl and under tray (L 578).

P 563. Hoare signed this tray (14) in a border and miter outline.

S 566. A tumbler with a Hoare signature.

C 564. A mayonnaise (9 D x 6 H) signed Hoare.

C 567. Hoare signed this vase.

S 569. A butter pat (3 D) with Hoare signature.

C 572. A jug (6.5 H) with a Hoare signature.

S 570. An individual salt (2.5 D) signed Hoare.

C 571. Hoare signed this vase (10.5 H).

C 568. A comport (7.5 D x 12 H) signed Hoare.

S 573. A comport (8 D x 8.5 H) signed Hoare.

C 574. Hoare signed this low bowl.

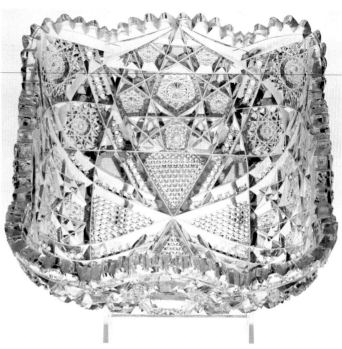

C 576. Hoare signed this square bowl (8 D).

C 577. A tray (11 x 6) has a Hoare signature.

L 578. An oval bowl (20 x 10 x 6) with underplate signed Hoare.

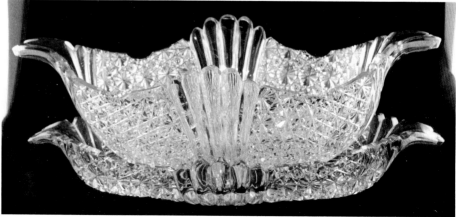

P 575. A decanter with neck rings and foot (6 D x 19.5 H)
        signed Hoare.

4. **Floral: flower and thistle, bowl (S 579)**

S 579. A bowl (8 D) signed Hoare combines daisies and thistles.

IRVING CUT GLASS COMPANY
Cutting Shop

Geometric Pattern
Combination Bars and Star: Elk (C 580).
Signed: mayonnaise bowl (C 581).

C 580. A bonbon (4 x 6) signed Irving in Elk Pattern.

C 581. A mayonnaise bowl (6 D x 4 H) with an Irving signature.

KRANTZ AND SMITH COMPANY
Cutting Shop

Geometric Pattern
Dual Motifs: celery (S 582).

S 582. A celery (11.1 x 4.5) by Krantz and Smith.

LACKAWANNA CUT GLASS COMPANY
Cutting Shop

Geometric Pattern
Pointed Loops: Iredel, tray (C 583).
Dual Motifs: Seneca, bowl (S 584).
Combination Bars and Star: Essen, square dish (S 585).
Combination Bars and Circles: Oakland (C 586).

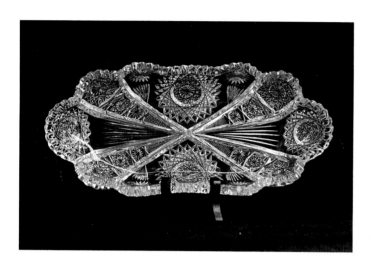

C 583. A tray in Iredel Pattern by Lackawanna and also signed Clark who later bought this company.

S 585. A square dish (10 D) by Lackawanna.

S 584. A relish (4 x 7.5) in Seneca Pattern by Lackawanna.

C 586. Oakland Pattern on a bowl (8 D) by Lackawanna.

LAUREL CUT GLASS COMPANY
Cutting Shop

Geometric Pattern
Dual Motifs: Amaranth, bowl (C 587); Cypress, bowl (S 588).
Floral: Crescent, whiskey tumbler (S 589).

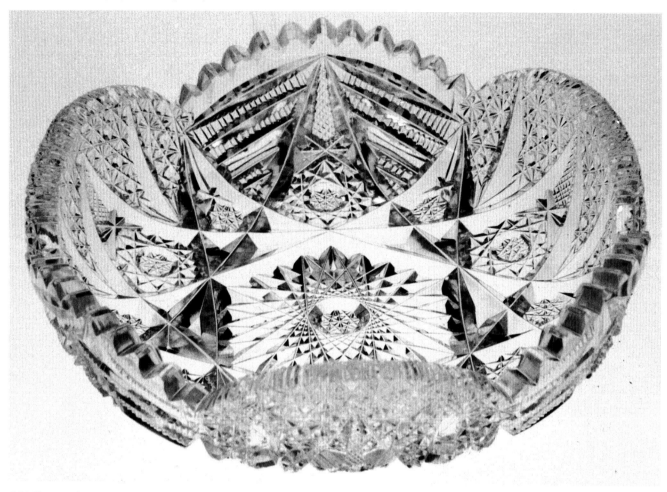

C 587. The Amaranth Pattern on a bowl (6 D) by Laurel Cut Glass Company.

C 588. A bowl (8 D) in Cypress Pattern by Laurel.

C 589. A whiskey tumbler in Crescent Pattern by Laurel.

L 590. An advertising device Libbey furnished to the stores that sold glass for it.

LIBBEY GLASS COMPANY
Factory
Advertising Device (L 590).

1. Geometric Pattern
Bars: Nassau, small plate (C 591).
Panels: Flute and Miter, tray (C 592).
Pointed Loops: Romano, bowl (C 593)
Dual Motifs: Mathilda, celery (C 594); X-ray, tray (C 595).

C 593. Libbey signed this bowl (9 D) in Romano Pattern.

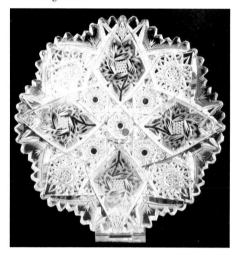

C 591. A small plate in Nassau Pattern signed Libbey.

C 592. A tray (15.5 D) in Pattern #136 signed Libbey.

C 594. The Mathilda Pattern in a celery (10 x 5.5) signed Libbey.

C 595. The X-Ray Pattern on a tray (13.5 D) signed Libbey.

2. Numbered Pattern

Rows: Pattern #36, small vase (S 596).
Border and Miter: Pattern #30, vase (S 597).
Dual Motifs: Pattern #39, cologne (S 598); Pattern #120, comport (S 599).

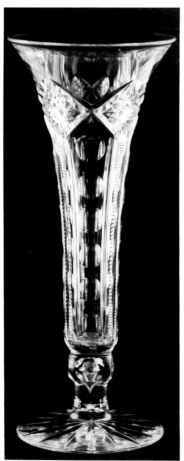

S 596. A vase (3 D x 5 H) in Pattern #36 by Libbey.

S 597. Libbey signed this vase (9.5 H) in Pattern #30.

S 598. Pattern #39 on a cologne identified by Libbey catalog.

S 599. A comport (7.5 D x 6 H) in Pattern #120 signed Libbey.

3. Signed Only

Pointed Loops: spoon tray (S 600); orange bowl (C 601).

Dual Motifs: whiskey jug, (C 602); tumbler (S 603); decanter (C 604); comport (S 605); whiskey jug (C 606); loving cup (C 607); bread tray (S 608).

Floral: vase (S 609).

S 600. This tray (5 x 6.5) has a Libbey signature.

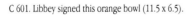

S 603. A whiskey tumbler (3.5 H) signed Libbey.

C 601. Libbey signed this orange bowl (11.5 x 6.5).

C 602. A whiskey jug (5 D x 7 H) signed Libbey.

C 604. Libbey signed this decanter (6.5 D x 7 H).

C 605. A comport (5.5 D x 6 H) signed Libbey.

C 606. A whiskey jug (4.5 D x 8 H) Libbey signed.

C 607. Libbey signed this
loving cup (6.5 H)

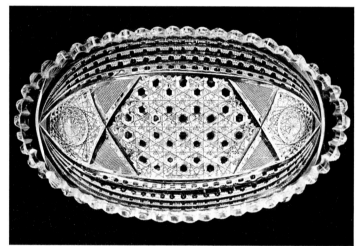

S 608. A bread tray (6.5 x 10.5) signed Libbey.

S 609. A vase (9.5 N) signed Libbey.

S 610. The Dorian Pattern on a bowl (9. 5 D) by Maple City.

S 611. The Cardinal Pattern on this tray (11.5 D) by Maple City.

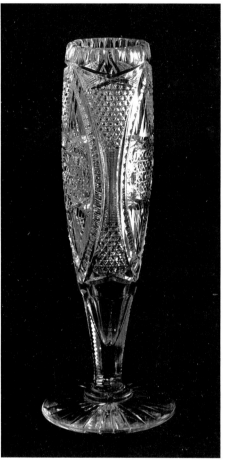

S 612. Maple City named the pattern Oxia on this tray (9 D).

MAPLE CITY GLASS COMPANY
Cutting Shop

1. Geometric Pattern
Bars: Dorian, bowl (S 610).
Star: Cardinal, plate (S 611); Oxia, plate (S 612),
Panels: Corsican, vase (C 613); Hebron, almond bowl (S 614).
Pointed Loops: Delphic, bonbon (S 615) ; Seward, celery (C 616).
Dual Motifs: Alcatic, bowl (S 617): Burton, plate (S 618); Delray, bowl (S 619); Dolphin jug (C 620); Onica, oil (S 621); Petrel, vase (P 622); Texal, jug (S 623).

C 613. The Corsican Pattern by Maple City on this vase.

S 614. The Hebron Pattern by Maple City on this butter pat (3 D).

S 615. A Maple City bonbon in the Delphic Pattern.

C 616. The celery (4 x 10) in Seward Pattern signed Maple City.

S 617. A bowl (8 D) in the Alsatia Pattern by Maple City.

S 618. A plate (7 D) in the Burton Pattern by Maple City.

S 619. The Delray Pattern on a bowl (8 D) by Maple City.

S 620. A Maple City jug (11.5 H) in Dolphin Pattern.

S 621. An oil in Onica Pattern by Maple City.

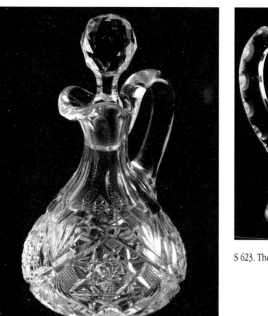

S 623. The Texel Pattern on a jug (8.5 H) by Maple City.

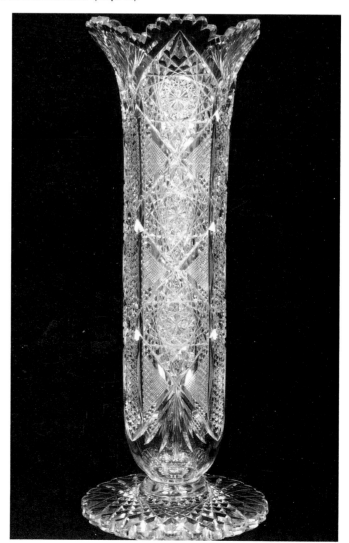

P 622. The Petrel Pattern by Maple City on this vase (6.5 D x 16 H).

2. Signed Only
Rows: covered butter and plate (S 624).
Dual Motifs: jug (S 625); jug (C 626).

S 624. A covered butter and plate by Maple City.

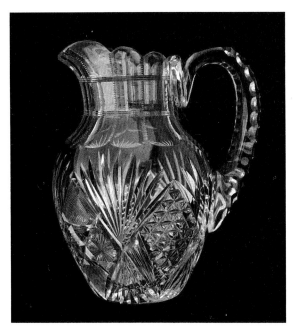

S 625. A jug (8 H) signed Maple City.

C 626. Maple City signed this jug (8 H).

MERIDEN CUT GLASS COMPANY
Cutting Shop

Geometric Pattern
Bars: Pattern #231F, small square plate (S 627); Pattern #125, bowl (S 628).
Border and Squares: Old Irish, jug (P 629).
Dual Motifs: Pattern #1650, footed celery (C 630).

S 627. Meriden Pattern #231 F on a plate (7 D).

P 629. The Old Irish Pattern on a jug (12.5) by Meriden.

S 628. Meriden Pattern #125 on a bowl (9 D).

C 630. A footed celery (11.5 x 6) in Pattern #1650 by Meriden.

S 631. The Nevada Pattern by C.F. Monroe on a carafe (9.5 H).

C. F. MONROE COMPANY
Cutting Department

Geometric Pattern
Border and Miter: Nevada, carafe (S 631); Prism, vase (C 632).
Star: Pattern #16, bowl (C 633).
Swirls: Ariel, vase (P 634)
Pointed Loops: Bellmere, jewel box (C 635); Nakara, jewel box (C 636).
Dual Motifs: lamp, signed on metal (P 637).

C 633. A bowl (9 D) in Pattern #16 by Monroe.

C 632. A vase (18 H) in Prism Pattern by C. F. Monroe.

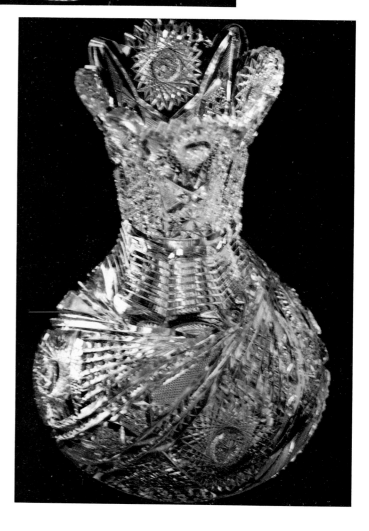

C 634. A vase (14 H) in the Ariel Pattern by Monroe.

C 635. Monroe signed the silver on this jewel box in the Bellmere Pattern.

C 636. The Nakara Pattern on a jewel box by Monroe.

P 637. A lamp (19 H) with Monroe hallmark on silver.

MT. WASHINGTON GLASS WORKS
Factory

Geometric Pattern
Rows: Russian, bowl (C 638); Strawberry-Diamond and Fan, bonbon (S 639); Three Cut Octagon, jug (C 640); Pattern #3, bowl (C 641).
Star: Bedford, square dish (C 642); Westminster, bowl (C 643).
Panels: Two Cut Octagon and Diamond, jug (C 644).
Dual Motifs: Pricilla, nappy (S 645).

S 639. A bonbon (8 x 13.5) by Mt. Washington in Strawberry-Diamond and Fan Pattern.

C 640. A jug (9 H) in 3 Cut Octagon Pattern by Mt. Washington.

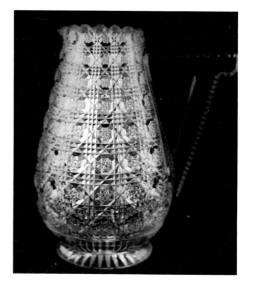

C 638. A square bowl (7 D) in Russian and Prism Pattern by Mt. Washington.

C 641. A bowl (10.5 D) in Pattern #3 by Mt Washington.

C 644. A Mt. Washington Pattern 2 Cut Octagon and Diamond on a jug (11.5 H).

C 642. Bedford Pattern on a square dish (5.5 D) by Mt. Washington.

C 643. Westminster Pattern on a bowl (4.5) by Mt. Washington.

C 645. A nappy (7 D) in Pricilla Pattern by Mt. Washington.

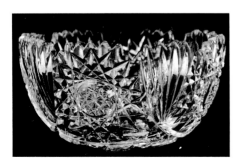

S 646. A bowl (5.5 D) signed by Newark Cut Glass Company.

NEWARK CUT GLASS COMPANY
Cutting Shop

Signed Only
Dual Motifs: bowl (S 646).

PAIRPOINT CORPORATION

Factory

1. Geometric Pattern

Rows: Dutch, tooth powders bottle (S 647): Savoy, basket (S 648).

Border and Miter: Angelus, vase (C 649) ; Brilliant, jug (C 650).

Dual Motifs: Berwick, cologne (C 651), Cactus, (S 652); Dauphin, jug (C 653); Duchess, bowl (S 654); Electra, bowl (S 655); Imperial, sugar and cream (S 656); Marigold, tray (C 657); Mavis, flower center (C 658); Meteor, comport (S 659); Urn & Flame, celery (C 660).

2. Floral

Daisy, glove box (C 661); Sillsbee, bowl (C 662);

3. Fruit, bowl (S 663).

S 647. Tooth powder bottle (4 H) in Dutch by Pairpoint.

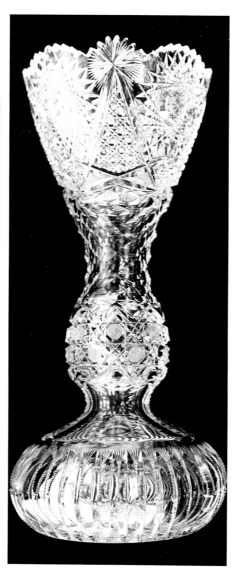

C 648. A basket (7 D) in Savoy Pattern by Pairpoint.

C 649. The Angelus Pattern by Pairpoint on a vase (14 H).

C 650. A jug (14 H) in Brilliant by Pairpoint.

C 651. A cologne (6.5 H) in Berwick by Pairpoint.

S 652. A vase (7 H) in Cactus Pattern by Pairpoint.

S 655. Pairpoint bowl (8 D) in Electric Pattern.

C 653. The Dauphin Pattern on a jug (10 H) by Pairpoint.

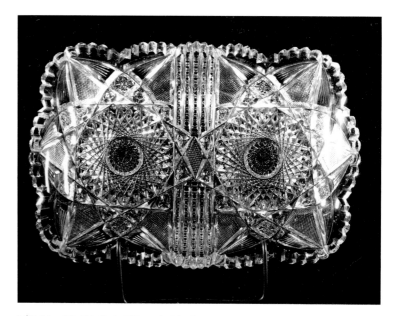

S 656. The Imperial Pattern on a sugar and cream set by Pairpoint.

S 657. A tray (12 x 8) in Marigold Pattern by Pairpoint.

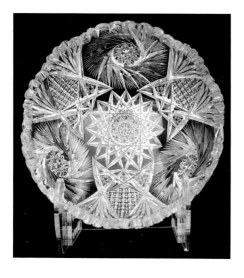

S 654. Duchess Pattern by Pairpoint on a bowl (8 D).

C 658. A flower center (14 D x 10 H) in Mavis Pattern by Pairpoint.

C 559. The Meteor Pattern by Pairpoint on this comport (6 D x 9 H).

C 660. Urn and Flame Pattern by Pairpoint on a celery (11 x 5).

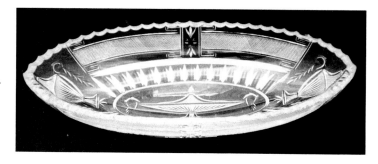

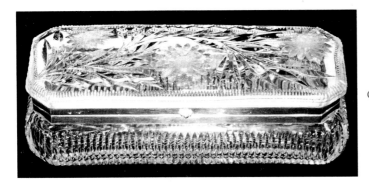

C 661 Pairpoint Daisy Pattern on a glove box (4 x 6 x 9).

C 662 Sillsbee Pattern by Pairpoint on a bowl (10 D), Patent #40,760.

C 663. A nappy bowl (7 D) in a floral pattern by Pairpoint.

F. X. PARSCHE AND SONS COMPANY
Cutting Shop

1. Geometric Pattern
Dual Motifs: Sunburst, sugar and cream (C 664).
2. Floral
Rows: floral amd geometric, plate (C 665).

C 664. Sunburst Pattern by F. X. Parsche on a sugar and cream set.

C 665. A plate (7.5 D) engraved by Parsche's grandfather.

PITKIN AND BROOKS
Cutting Shop

1. Geometric Pattern
Bars: Prince, small plate (C 666).
Rows: King George, cologne (S 667).
Border and Miter: Aurora Borealis, vase (C 668); Prism, vase (C 669).
Panels: Empress, vase (C 670)
Dual Motifs: Byrno, sugar and cream (C 671); Keystone, punch bowl (C 672); Lustre, celery (S 673); Star, whiskey bottle (C 674); Winona, bowl (C 675); Pattern #647 , salt and pepper (C 676).

C 666. Prince Pattern by Pitkin & Brooks on a plate (7 D).

S 667. A cologne (8.15 H) signed by P & B in the King George Pattern.

C 668. A vase (12 H) by P & B in the Aurora Borealis Pattern.

C 669. A vase (7 H) in the Prism Pattern by P & B.

C 670. The Empress Pattern by P & B on this vase (14.5 H).

C 671. A sugar and cream in the Byrns Pattern by P & B.

C 672. The Keystone Pattern on a punch bowl (10 D x 9 H) by P & B.

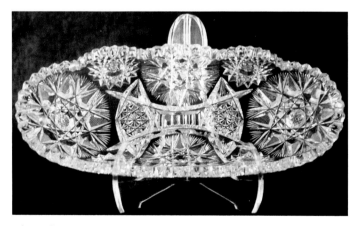

S 673. A celery (11) in Lustre Pattern by P & B.

C 674. P & B whiskey bottle (11.5 H) in Star Pattern.

C 676. Salt and pepper set in pattern #647_ by P & B.

C 675. The Winona Pattern by P & B on a bowl (8 D).

2. Signed Only
Border and Strawberry-Diamond and Fan: punch bowl (C 677).
Dual Motifs: oil (C 678).

C 677. A punch bowl signed P & B.

C 678. An oil with a P & B signature.

QUAKER CITY CUT GLASS COMPANY
Cutting Shop

Geometric Pattern
Circles: Columbia, bowl (C 679); DuBerry, jug (C 680).
Dual Motifs: Wallace, bowl (S 681).

C 680. A jug (10.5 H) in DuBerry Pattern by Quaker City.

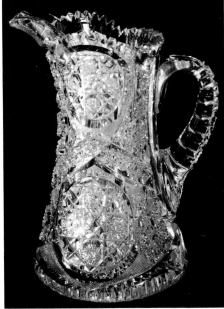

C 679. A bowl (9 D) in Columbia Pattern by Quaker City.

S 681. The Wallace Pattern by Quaker City on a bowl (8 D).

H. P. SINCLAIRE AND COMPANY
Cutting Shop

1. Geometric Pattern
Rows: Antique No. 1 E Engr., bowl (C 682).
Border and Miter: Cornwall, tray (P 683);
Diamond and Silver Threads, clock (C 684).
Swirls: Buffalo, napkin ring (S 685).
Dual Motifs: Constellation, punch bowl (P 686); Idaho, punch bowl (P 687).

C 682. Sinclaire named this pattern on a bowl (10 D) Antique NO.1 E Engr.

C 684. A clock (4 H) in Diamonds and Silver Threads Pattern by Sinclaire.

P 683. A tray (15 D) in Cornwall Pattern by Sinclaire.

S 685. The Buffalo Pattern by Sinclaire on a napkin holder.

P 686. A signed punch bowl (18 D x 11.5 H) in Constellation Pattern by Sinclaire.

P 687. A punch bowl (18 D x 11 H) in Idaho Pattern by Sinclaire.

C 688. A clock (4 H) signed Sinclaire.

C 689. A plate (10 D) signed Sinclaire.

C 690. A car vase (71 H) in Lafayette Pattern signed Sinclaire.

2. Signed Only
Rows: Clock (C 688).
Border and Flowers: bowl (C 689)
.3. Floral and Geometrics Pattern
Rows: Lafayette, car vase (S 690).
Border and Flutes: Stratford, covered jar (C 691).
Pointed Loops: handkerchief box (C 692).
Dual Motifs: Fuchia, handkerchief box (S 693); Pattern #40, candlesticks (C 694); Stars, Hollows & Engr., tray (C 695).

C 691. A covered comport (6 D x 13.5 H) in Stratford by Sinclaire.

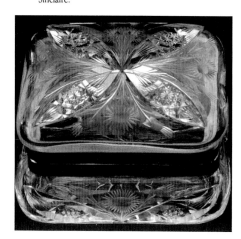

C 692. Sinclaire produced this handkerchief box (6 D).

C 695. Sinclaire named the pattern on this tray Stars, Hollows, and Engr.

S 693. A handkerchief box signed by Sinclaire in the Fuschia Pattern.

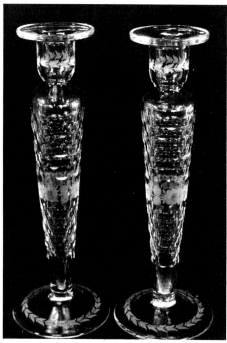

C 694. Candlesticks (11 H) in #40 Pattern by Sinclaire.

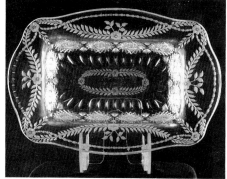

4. Floral
Aster, vase (C 696); Engraved Roses, vase (S 697); signed tray (P 698); signed bowl (S 699)
.5. Scene
Pheasant, tray (P 700); Deer, tray (P 701)

S 699. A bowl signed Sinclaire.

C 697. A vase (9.5 H) in Engraved Roses by Sinclaire.

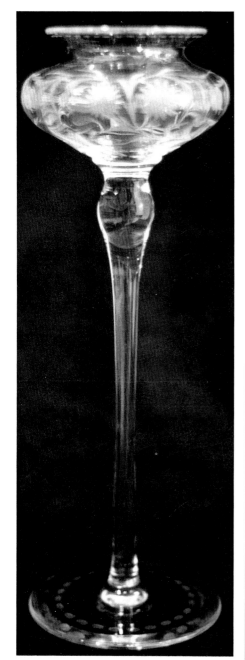

C 696. Vase (12 H) in Aster Pattern by Sinclaire.

P 698. A tray (14 D) signed Sinclaire.

P 700. Oval tray (9 D) in Pheasant Pattern by Sinclaire.

P 701. Deer Pattern by Sinclaire.

STERLING Cut Glass Company
Cutting Shop

Geometric Pattern
Dual Motifs: Arcadia, tray (C 702).

C 702. Arcada Pattern by Sinclaire.

L. STRAUS AND SONS
Cutting Shop

1. Geometric Pattern
Bars: Norma, bowl (C 703).
Panels: Electra, rose globe (C 704).
Gothic Arch: Ducal, bowl (S 705).
Pointed Loops: Rex, small plate (S 706) .
Dual Motifs: Antoinette, tray (S 707)

S 705. A bowl (8 D) signed by Straus in Ducal Pattern.

C 703. Norma Pattern by Straus on this bowl (8 D).

S 706. A plate (7 D) in Rex Pattern by Straus.

C 704 Electra Pattern on this rose globe (5.5 x 5.5) by Straus.

S 707. Antoinette Pattern by Straus on a plate (7 D).

2. Signed Only
Puntes and Miters: bowl (C 708).
Star: bowl (C 709).
Swirls: bowl (C 710).
Pointed Loops: bowl (C 711); covered butter and plate (C 712).
Dual Motifs: covered butter and plate (C 713); whiskey jug (C 714); decanter (C 715).

C 708. A bowl (9 D) signed Straus.

C 709. A signed Straus bowl (9 D).

C 710. A bowl (8 D) signed Straus.

C 711. A bowl (9 D) with a Straus signature.

C 712. A covered butter and plate signed Straus.

C 713. A covered butter and plate with Straus signature.

C 714. A jug (16 H) signed
Straus.

C 715. A decanter (16 H) Straus signed.

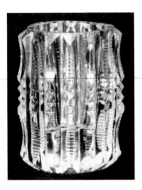

S 716. A Taylor Brothers catalog
pictured this toothpick
holder.

TAYLOR BROTHERS
Cutting Shop

Geometric Pattern
Miters: tooth pick (S 716).
Dual Motifs: Cornell, whiskey bottle (C 717); Dawson, mug (C 718)

TUTHILL CUT GLASS COMPANY
Cutting Shop

Signed Only
Dual Motifs: bowl (C 719).
Flowers and Geometrics: vase (C 720); bonbon (C 721); vase (C 722); comport (C 723).
Floral Only: Tiger Lily, vase (C 724),
Fruit: Blackberry, tray (C 725); clusters, tray (C 726).

C 718. The Dawson Pattern on a handled tumbler
by Taylor Brothers.

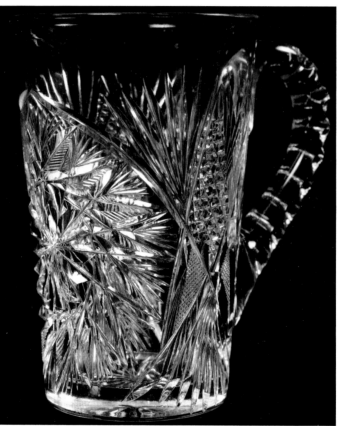

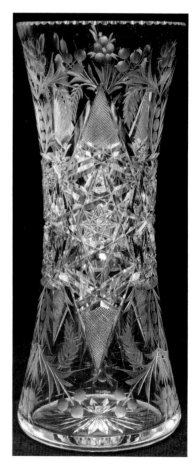

C 717. The Cornell Pattern on a
whiskey bottle (12 H) by Taylor
Brothers.

C 720. Tuthill signed this vase (10 H).

C 719. A bowl (8 D) signed Tuthill.

C 721. A relish with a Tuthill signature.

C 724. An urn in Tiger Lily by Tuthill.

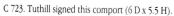

C 723. Tuthill signed this comport (6 D x 5.5 H).

C 725. Blackberry Pattern on this tray (12 D) by Tuthill.

S 726. An oval tray signed Tuthill.

C 722. A vase (10 H) signed Tuthill.

UNGER BROTHERS
Cutting Shop

Geometric Pattern
Star: Florodora, nappy (S 727).

S 727. A nappy (6 D) in Florodora by Unger.

WILCOX SILVER PLATE COMPANY
Silver and Cut Glass Shop

Signed on Silver
Border and Miter (S 728).
Dual Motifs: sugar shaker (S 729); sugar shaker (S 730).

S 729. A sugar shaker (5.5 H) Wilcox signed on the silver.

S 730. The sterling silver lid on this sugar shaker has a Wilcox hallmark.

S 728. Wilcox signed the silver on this candlestick (9.5 H).

CANADIAN
Gowans, Kent and Company. Ltd.R

Floral and Geometric Pattern: celery (S 731).

Gundy, Clapperton Company

Dual Motifs: nappy (S 732)

Roden Brothers

Geometric Pattern
Star: Royal, bowl (S 733)
Dual Motifs: Aster, celery (C 734); Oakland, jug (C 735); Regina, puff box (C 736); Pattern #307, comport (C 737).

C 735. The Oakland Pattern on this jug by Roden Brothers.

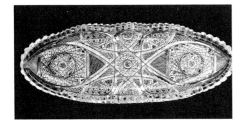

S 731. A celery by Gowans, Kent & Company, Ltd.

S 732. Gundy-Clapperton Company signed this nappy (6 D).

C 734. Aster Pattern on this celery (11.5 x 4) by Roden Brothers.

C 736. The Regina pattern by Roden Brothers on this puff box (4 D x 3.5 H).

S 733. A nappy bowl (8 D) in Royal Pattern by Roden Brothers.

C 737. A comport (9 D x 6.25 H) in Pattern #307 by Roden Brothers.

C 738. Georgia Pattern by Higgins and Seiter on a whiskey bottle (14 H).

WHOLESALE, AGENT, OR STORE

1. Higgins and Seiter
Agent
Geometric Pattern
Dual Motifs: Georgia, whiskey bottle (C 738).

2. G. W. Huntley
Wholesale
Geometric Pattern
Bars: Stratford, jug (C 739).
Dual Motifs: Norway, napkin ring (S 740).

3. Marshall Field and Company
Department Store
Geometric Pattern
Circles: Pattern #70130, orange bowl (C 741).
Dual Motifs: Pattern #70426, bowl (P 742); Pattern #71524, nappy (S 743); Pattern #76003, mayonnaise (S 744).
Combination Border and Loops: bowl (C 745).

S 740. Norway Pattern (right) by G. W. Huntley on a napkin ring and Jet Pattern (left) by Bergen.

Any identifications by pattern or signature of cut glass increases the value. So knowledge does add another dividend to the excitement of discovery.

C 739. G. W. Huntley jug (12 H) in Stratford Pattern.

S 743. Pattern #71524 by Marshall Field & Company on a nappy (6 D).

C 741. Orange Bowl (4 x 5 x 8) by Marshall Field & Company in Pattern #70130.

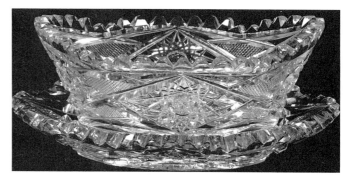

S 744. A mayonnaise in Pattern #76003 by Marshall Field & Company.

P 742. A square bowl (8 D) by Marshall Field & Company in Pattern #70426.

C 745. A bowl (9 D) by Marshall Field Company.

CHAPTER 9 *American Colored Glass*

All cut glass has increased in value, but colored pieces have gone up the most. For one reason, colored pieces represent only a small percentage of total cut glass production in the United States. Further, both collector and dealer want American colored cut glass and not European.

No information specifically describes the features pertaining to American colored glass. But making deductions from accepted facts can suggest possible characteristics.

BASIC FACTS

Information from old catalogs, advertisements in magazines of the Brilliant Era, and patent records provide much of this information. Interviews with craftsmen who cut colored glass and descendants of company owners added other facts. From these make your deduction.

1. Dating the Period

Estimating the time span for production of colored glass can provide clues for deductions. The Strawberry-Diamond and the Russian Patterns represent early colored cut glass. Take the example of the Russian Pattern patented in June, 1882. These Russian pieces indicate a simple beginning (L 746), the increase in the amount of color (L 747), and finally an ornate example that increased the amount of color on the stopper, handle, neck, and foot (L 748). This last example indicated that the period lasted a few years after the turn of the century.

So generally speaking you can deduce the period started at the beginning of the 1880s. By the middle of the 1880s Boston and Sandwich Glass Company tried to cure financial difficulties by producing colored cut glass. The period finally ended near the height of the geometric cutting, shortly after the turn of the century.

L 746. A cranberry overlay on a decanter (13.5 H) in Russian Pattern where color does not cover the handle, foot, or stopper, a piece cut early in the period.

L 747. The cranberry overlay on a jug (8 5 H) where the Russian Pattern covers more of the neck, the lip, the handle, and border on the body, indicating a later time period.

L 748. The cranberry overlay on this decanter (12.5 H) added more color to the handle, the stopper, and a foot. These indicated the latest years in production.

You can not give specific dates. No information exists in regard to how soon after the company received the patent that the piece appeared in color. In fact, patent records do not mention colored cut glass. Although a dated catalog illustrates a duplicate of the colored piece, no one knows how much time passed between the catalog date and the production in color.

2. Types of Colored Glass

American companies produced three types of colored cut glass. The most popular consisted of color-cut-to-clear made with an overlay (L 749). The blower started work with a gob of molten glass for a clear blank. At a certain stage a worker took the blank to a pot containing a colored metal. He gave the blank a heavy coat of color. Then the blower took over again and produced the full shape. If you look at the edge of a colored overlay, you can see a distinct line that divides the color from the clear.

Do not confuse overlay with flashed or cased glass. In flashed glass, the workman merely dipped the blank in color which fuses with the clear. This color will wear off with heavy usage. Cased glass consisted of two layer of blown glass as in art glass.

Americans produced very little solid colored pieces. The factory used the solid color mostly for small pieces as a knife rest (L 750) or small wines (L 751). After the 1900s Dorflinger enameled solid colored wines (L 752). Europeans also used enamel, so make sure that the general designs contains American motifs.

In the 1920s several glass companies engraved solid colored glass on thin blanks. This type of glass does not form a part of the Brilliant Period (L 753).

L 751. A solid ruby color except on the base of the foot on a wine.

L 752. A solid ruby wine with added enamel by Dorflinger.

L 749. Three colognes in basic green overlay.

L 750. A solid amber color on a knife rest.

L 753. A cranberry cracker and cheese shape in Engraved Grapes Pattern by Pairpoint on a solid, thin blank, typical of the 1920s.

3. Production Companies.

The New England Glass Company which later became Libbey produced some color-cut-to-clear shapes (L 754). The type of motifs and shape of the piece some erroneously associate with Dorflinger. Dorflinger did produce the same shape with neck rings and the exact stopper but in a different pattern. No material available on Dorflinger shows this particular pattern. Warning, before you jump to a conclusion, make sure you have checked all available facts.

Dorflinger, Mt. Washington, Fry, and Libbey made colored blanks for cutting shops. They also cut colored cut glass. Shops that repeated their clear patterns on colored glass included Hawkes, Hoare, Bergen, and Clark. Pairpoint did produce colored cut glass other than the previously mention engraved type. So when you try to identify a piece of color-cut-to-clear glass, begin with these companies.

4. Colors Tones

American basic colors included green, ruby (L 755), blue (L 756), amethyst, and amber (L 757). Other shades developed from these basic ones: from ruby came cranberry (L 558), green provided aqua, and amber became yellow. Colors resulted from the addition of various oxides to the clear molten metal and the length of time the piece stayed in the colored solution.

L 754. A decanter (8.5 H) in green by the New England Glass Company.

L 757. An amber wine in Hob Diamond by Dorflinger.

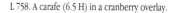

L 758. A carafe (6.5 H) in a cranberry overlay.

L 755. Wines in ruby and in green cut by Dorflinger in the Strawberry-Diamond and Fan Pattern.

L 756. A bell (7 H) with a blue overlay in Strawberry-Diamond and Fan.

Oxides of cobalt, copper, antimony, and manganese produced the blue overlay. Carbon, sulphur, iron, chromium, uranium provided the amber coat. Chromium or protoxide of copper, iron, and uranium turned the glass green. Ruby developed from the oxide of gold or suboxide of copper.

At the end of the day, the workmen could use the leftover colored metal in the pots to blow pieces for their own used. Supposedly "rainbow" glass started this way as seen in a pattern called Hob Diamond by Dorflinger (L 759). The workman dipped the start of a blank into different colors: ruby, green, or amber (L 760) to produce the rainbow. Most of the pieces basically have three colors.

For color-cut-to-clear, the American usually used a one color overlay, but you always find exceptions as with this jug in Russian (L 761) by the New England Glass Company containing ruby, amber, and blue. This smelling salt bottle has ruby and amber with a sterling silver top (L 762). A collector owns a loving cup in the Crystal City Pattern by Hoare. The craftsman overlaid the clear glass first with a coat of blue and later added one of ruby. Then he cut through to the clear.

The Empire Cut Glass Company, owned by Fry, experimented with blanks in amber and blue. The glass may contain a blue base, blue or amber handles, or a half blue and half amber bowl. The Success Pattern appeared on the original designs. When the company closed, Louis Iorio, the head of the cutting department, sold a number of the unused blanks to the employees and purchased many for himself. His later cuttings differed from the early geometric pattern because of the additions of engraved flowers (L 763).

L 759. An ink well (3.5 D x 2.5 H) in rainbow.

L 761. A jug (12 H) by New England Glass Company combines blue, amber, and ruby in the Russian Pattern.

L 762. A smelling salt bottle (6 H) with a sterling silver top in ruby and amber.

L 763. A relish (4 x 8) cut later with flowers by Louis Iorio on a Fry blank.

L 760. A rainbow decanter (14 H) in cranberry, amber, and green.

L 764. A cranberry decanter (9 H) in Flute Pattern by Clark.

5. Identification

Your main source of identification consists of matching the pattern on the colored piece to a clear one. Generally, a company tended to color those patterns which proved popular in clear cut glass. Only an 1892 Hawkes catalog offered to cut a Russian Pattern in color. Out of 135 catalogs, only this one offers to cut a colored piece of glass.

Very few companies signed the colored cut glass. Hawkes signed a piece cut in the Chrysanthemum Pattern. Both Hawkes and Libbey signed pieces cut in the Strawberry-Diamond and Fan. Clark signed a decanter in the Flute Pattern. A carafe contained a Fry signature. So you can conclude that very few companies signed color-cut-to-clear glass.

IDENTIFIED PATTERNS

Careful research has identified the E patterns in colored cut glass.

1. T. B. Clark and Company
Geometric Pattern
Panels: Flute, cranberry decanter, (L 764).
Dual Motifs: Patent #16,720, cranberry claret (L 765).
2. C. Dorflinger and Sons
Geometric Pattern
Rows: Strawberry-Diamond, aqua claret (L 766); Old Colony, green whiskey bottle (L 767).
Border and Miter: signed on silver, decanter (L 768).

L 765. A cranberry claret signed Clark in Patent #16,720.

L 766. An aqua claret in Strawberry-Diamond by Dorflinger.

L 768. A cranberry jug (11.5) signed on the sterling silver by Dorflinger.

L 767. An aqua whiskey bottle (11.5 H) in Old Colony Pattern by Dorflinger.

Border and cane: Pattern #129, also signed on silver (L 769).
Swirls: cranberry wine, (L 770).
Dual Motifs: Savoy, three steps in cutting green (L 771), cranberry (L 772), green (L 773); Sultana on cigar jar (L 774); Pattern #50, cranberry wine (L 775).

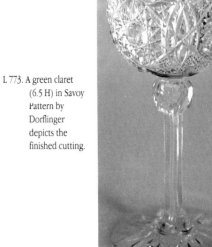

L 773. A green claret (6.5 H) in Savoy Pattern by Dorflinger depicts the finished cutting.

L 769. Pattern #129 in ruby on a vase (13 H) by Dorflinger with a Shreve hallmark on the sterling silver.

L 771. A green claret (6.5 H) in Savoy Pattern by Dorflinger that shows the first step in cutting.

L 774. A green cigar jar (5.5 D x 9 H) in the Sultana Pattern by Dorflingler.

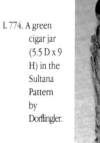

L 772. A cranberry claret (6.5 H) in Savoy Pattern by Dorflinger pictures the second step in cutting.

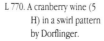

L 770. A cranberry wine (5 H) in a swirl pattern by Dorflinger.

L 775. Pattern #50 by Dorflinger on a cranberry claret (6.5 H).

L 776. A floral cranberry vase (12 H) in Pattern #16 by Dorflinger.

Floral
Pattern #16, cranberry vase (L 776); Stone Engr. 2, small loving cup (L 777).
3. T. G. Hawkes and Company
Geometric Pattern
Border and Miter: Brunswick, footed ruby rose globe (L 778); Marquis, green decanter (L 779).
Dual Motifs: Gladys, ruby nappy (L 780); Norwood, cranberry claret (L 781); Valencia, turquoise bowl (L 782); Venetian, green vase (L 783)

Signed
Cranberry claret (L 784); mirror on foot (L 785).
4. J. Hoare and Company
Geometric Pattern

L 779. A green decanter (11.5 H) in Marquis Pattern by Hawkes.

L 777. A cranberry loving cup (2.5 D x 3 H) in Pattern Stone Engr. 2 by Dorflinger.

L 780. A ruby nappy (7 D) in Gladys Pattern by Hawkes.

L 778. A ruby footed rose globe (6 D x 7 H) in Brunswick Pattern signed by Hawkes.

L 781. Hawkes cut this cranberry wine (5 H)
in the Norwood Pattern.

L 783. Hawkes produced this green vase (12 H) in the
Venetian Pattern.

L 782. A turquoise bowl (8 D) in the Valencia Pattern by Hawkes.

L 784. A cranberry claret identified from a clear piece by
Hawkes.

L 785. A mirror on a stand (12.5 H) cut in green and signed by
Hawkes.

Rows: Russian, cranberry basket (L 786); Russian and Fan, cranberry claret (L 787).
Dual Motifs: Acme, cranberry claret (L 788).
5. Libbey Glass Company
Geometric Pattern
Panels: Flute, green whiskey jug (L 789).
Dual Motifs: Imperial, ruby claret (L 790).
6. Mt. Washington Glass Works
Geometric Pattern
Rows: Prince, amber claret (L 791).
Panels: Regent, ruby jug (L 792).
Dual Motifs: Bedford, green vase (L 793). .

L 786. A ruby basket (8.5 D x 7.5 H) cut in Persian by Hoare.

L 788. Hoare cut this cranberry claret in the Acme
Pattern.

L 787. A cranberry wine (4.5 H) in Russian and Fan
by Hoare.

L 789. The Flute Pattern by Libbey on this green jug (7.5 H).

L 790. A ruby claret (5 H) by Libbey in the Imperial Pattern.

L 791. An amber claret (5.5 H) in the Prince Pattern by Mt. Washington

L 792. A ruby jug (13.5 H) in the Regent Pattern by Mt. Washington.

L 793. Mt. Washington cut the Bedford Pattern on this green vase (5 D x 14 H).

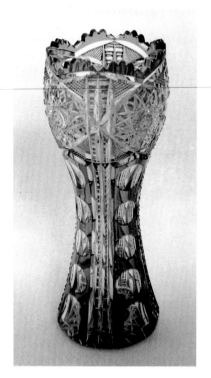

L 794. A green vase (11 H) in the Henrietta Pattern by Pairpoint.

7. Pairpoint Corporation
Geometric Pattern
Border and Puntes: Henrietta, green vase (L 794).
8. Boston and Sandwich Glass Company
Geometric Pattern
Rows: Octagon Diamond, four ruby colognes (L 795); Sharp Diamond, amber cologne (L 796);
Strawberry-Diamond and Fan, cranberry cologne (L 797);
Panels and Stars, ruby cologne (L 798).
9. L. Straus and Sons

L 796. The Sharp Diamond Pattern by Sandwich on this solid amber cologne.

L 797. The Strawberry-Diamond and Fan Pattern by Sandwich on a cranberry cologne (5 H).

L 795. Four ruby colognes in the Octagon Diamond Pattern by Sandwich.

L 798. A ruby cologne (5 H) in Panels and Stars by Sandwich.

Dural Motifs: Imperial, cranberry claret (L 799); ruby Rhine wine (L 800).

UNIDENTIFIED PATTERNS

Geometric Pattern
Rows: Strawberry-Diamond, ruby claret (L 801); blue claret (L 802); Strawberry-Diamond and Fan, (L 803); ruby claret with punties (L 804); amber goblet (L 805); green flower globe (L 806); cranberry finger bowl (L 807).
Border and Miter: cranberry wine decanter (L 808).
Gothic Arch: green mug (L 809).
Panels: ruby vase (L 810).
Dual Motifs: ruby bell (L 811); blue bowl (L 812) ruby low bowl (L 813); ruby bowl (L 814); cranberry carafe (L 815); green cologne (L 816); ruby comport (L 817); blue decanter (L 818); cranberry decanter (L 819); ruby flower globe (L 820); ruby jug (L 821); green jug (L 822); green jug (L 823); green loving cup (L 824); cranberry chalice (L 825); cranberry claret (L 826); cranberry claret (L 827); green vase (L 828).

L 799. A cranberry claret in
Imperial Pattern by
Straus.

L 800. A ruby Rhine wine by
Straus.

L 802. A blue claret in
Strawberry-Diamond Pattern
with wide border.

L 801. A ruby claret in
Strawberry-Diamond Pattern
with a wide border.

L 803. An amber claret in
Strawberry-Diamond and Fan.

L 804. A ruby claret (5.5 H) in rows of puntes.

L 806. A green flower globe (5 D x 5.5 H) in a rows outline.

L 808. A cranberry wine decanter (16 H).

L 807. A cranberry finger bowl and plate.

L 805. An amber goblet in a rows outline.

L 809. A green mug (3 D x 4.5 H).

L 811. A bell with a ruby overlay.

L 810. A ruby vase (14 H) in a panel outline.

L 812. A blue bowl in a dual motifs outline.

L 813. A low bowl in a ruby overlay.

L 815. A cranberry carafe (4.5 D x 7 H).

L 814. A ruby bowl (9 D).

L 816. A cologne (5.5 H) in green.

L 817. A comport with a ruby overlay.

L 819. A cranberry decanter (9 H) in simple styling.

L 818. A blue decanter with
matching stopper.

L 820. A footed rose globe in a ruby overlay.

L 821. A ruby overlay on a jug (9 H).

L 823. A green jug (10 H) with a Tiffany hallmark on the sterling silver.

L 822. A green jug (11 H) with a flat base.

L 824. A loving cup (7.5 D x 8 H) with a green overlay.

L 825. A chalice (11 H) in a dual motifs outline.

L 826. A claret (4.5 H) with a
cranberry overlay.

L 827. A cranberry claret (4.5 H).

L 828. A green vase (10 H) with a bulbous shape.

Floral Pattern
Green decanter (L 829); cranberry jug (L 830); cranberry whiskey tumbler (L 831).

L 830. A geometric border and engraving on a cranberry jug (10.5 H) with a silver rim.

L 829. A green decanter (12.5 H) cut in a thistle pattern.

L 831. A cranberry whiskey tumbler (3.5 H) combines swirls with flowers.

FOREIGN COLORED GLASS

Within recent years catalogs from Cristalleries Du Val Saint-Lampert for 1906 and 1908 have come to the attention of dealers and collectors. The catalogs give no names, only numbers. Some patterns look very American. This bowl illustrated in the catalog as Pattern #44 (L 832) looks very American in design. In fact one collector who has a copy of the Val St. Lambert catalog said that he found thirty illustrations that duplicated those of American cut glass. For example, Clark named this pattern on a green vase Iris but Val St. Lambert called it Pattern #54 (L 833). These foreign catalogs do not show the patterns in color. In looking at actual pieces from foreign companies, you will notice slight differences in the shades of color from that of Americans. These companies, however, duplicate American shapes as well.

By all means observe any display of colored cut glass and notice the shapes and tones of colors. See if you can make any deduction of identification using the previous information. Such deductions make you more aware of the characteristics of American colored cut glass.

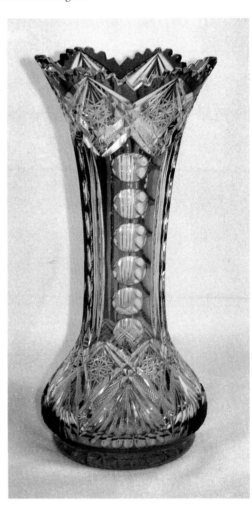

L 832. A ruby orange bowl pictured in a Val St. Lambert catalog as Pattern #44.

833. A green vase (12.5 H) called Iris by Clark and Pattern #54 by Val St. Lambert catalog.

CHAPTER 10 *The Unidentified*

Both collectors and dealers have sent good pictures of choice pieces of cut glass. We can not identify them with the research material we own. A number of the unknown patterns look so very good we have decided to include them in a chapter of pictures only in this book.

Perhaps you know some of the patterns or the companies that produced them. If you can identify any, send us the number of the illustration, the name of the pattern or the company, and especially the source of your identification. Hopefully we can include any new identifications with the next printing of this book.

To make identification easier we have arranged the pictures in alphabetical order by shapes and have pointed out any unique feature of the piece.

C 834. A bonbon (6.5 x 4.5) contains a looped handle in the center.

C 836. This low bowl (8 D) uses a gothic arch to leave no space uncut.

C 837. The ornate cutting on the diversified panels of this square bowl (8 D) makes it exceptional.

C 835. This low bowl (8 D) develops the pattern around a star outline that blends with the crimped rim.

C 838. A combination of pointed loops and circles outline accent the crimped shape.

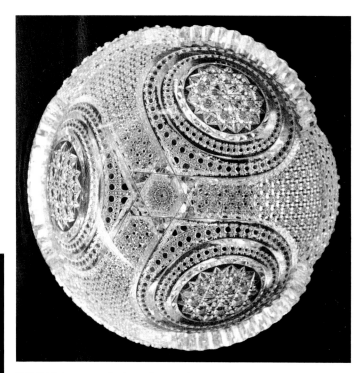

P 841. Triple frames around a cluster of stars result in an interesting pattern on this bowl (9 D).

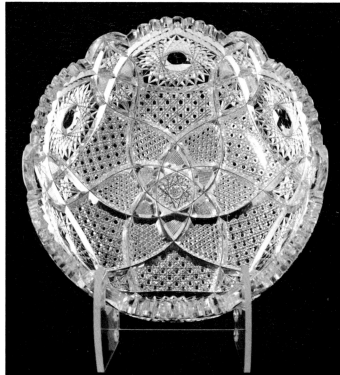

P 839. The star outline in the center and the hobstars with clear centers make this bowl (9 D) unusual.

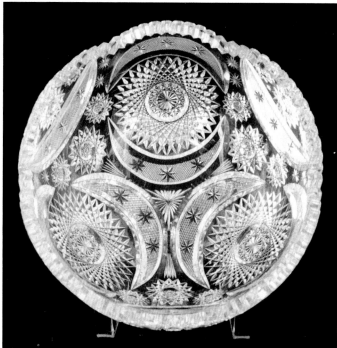

P 842. Complete cutting of this bowl (9 D) results from a combination of new moons and stars.

C 840. The notched rims that form the circles for the pinstars dominate this bowl (9 D).

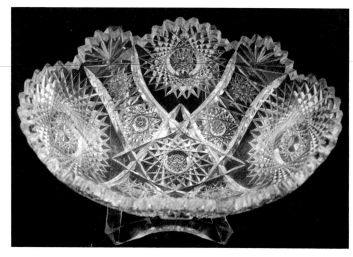

C 845. Bars and large hobstars on the fruit bowl (10 x 7) create a bold pattern.

C 843. Feathered loops of cane and a four square center create an excellent pattern on this bowl (9 D).

C 844. The oval shape and modernistic butterfly attract attention to this fruit bowl (9 x 7.5).

P 846. The oval shape and combination of bars and rows miter outline make the fruit bowl (10.5 x 9) very choice.

C 847. The exactness of the pattern on this punch bowl (10 D x 14 H) makes it remarkable.

C 848. The combination of geometric pointed loops and flowers make this handkerchief box (6 D) very choice.

C 850. The star miter outline and hobstars give this jewel box (8 D) an excellent balance.

C 851. The swirling motifs on the top and the base of this jewel box (5 D) make it outstanding.

C 849. The pointed loop on this handkerchief box (7 D) offers a contrast to the square shape.

S 852. Two candlestick sets (9 H & 10 H) in exactly the same pattern emphasize the unusual.

C 853. The simplicity and balance of this celery pattern (11 x 4) make it exceptional.

C 854. This celery (12 x 4) has an outstanding pattern.

C 855. This celery (11.5 x 6.5) shows a rhythm in the pattern.

C 856. The shape of the cologne (7.5 H) emphasizes the fans and hobstars.

L 857. Three features make this flower pot (6.5 D x 5 H) exceptional: Russian Pattern, the function, and the sterling silver lining.

C 858. The sterling silver lid, the handles, and the engraved strawberries make this dish (7 D x 3.5 H) remarkable.

C 859. The square shape of the tobacco jar (5 D by 8.5 H) creates a unique piece.

C 861. The blending of the panels with the unique shape gives it a plus.

C 860. This tanker (12 H) balances the pattern with the shape.

C 862. The two pointed panels that alternate and fit the shape of this jug (8.5 H) provide a distinctive piece of cut glass.

C 863. The alternating panels and hobstar border show unusual balance in the pattern on this tanker (11.5 H).

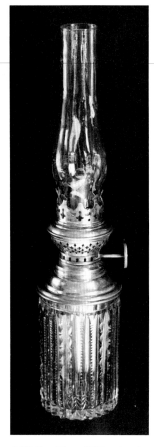

C 865. The oil lamp (12 H) catches the interest of any buyer.

C 866. The shape, handle and pattern make this oil lamp (13 H) most remarkable.

S 864. The flat rim and simplicity of pattern understate the beauty of this jug (7 H).

C 867. The Trellis Pattern frames a single fruit on this nappy (6 D) and places it in a choice category.

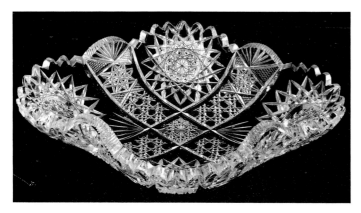

S 868. The bars blend with crimped shape and hobstars to form an outstanding relish (7.5 x 5.5).

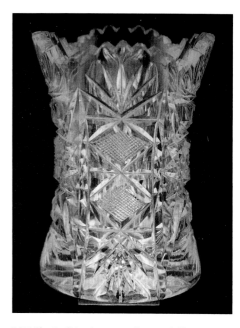

S 871. The simplicity of pattern on this spoonholder (5 H) attracts attention.

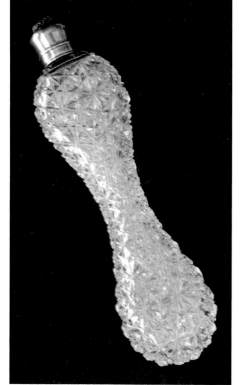

S 869. An unusual shape on a smelling salts bottle in Russian Pattern.

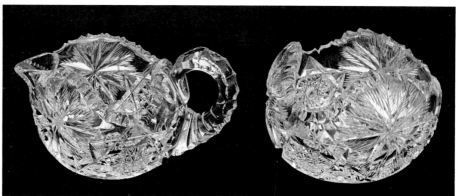

C 872. The flashed star in the pattern and the handless sugar make this set choice.

S 870. The contrast in motifs on this spoon tray (8 x 4) proves rather startling.

P 873. The outstanding pattern on this tray (18 x 10.5) places it in the top category.

P 874. An exceptional tray with detailed motifs in the pattern.

P 875. This tray (10 x 7.5) has remarkable balance between the bars and the large hobstar.

C 876. An outstanding tray (18 x 10.5) in a pointed loops outline.

C 877. The border of 8-point stars frames this 48-point hobstar in the base center of the tray (13 D).

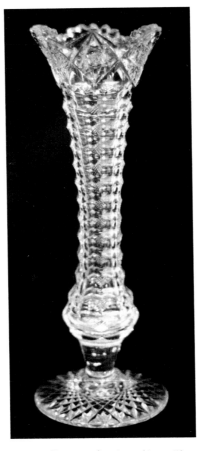

C 878. An effective use of punties on this vase (12 H).

C 879. A vase (19.5 H) rates the remarkable category.

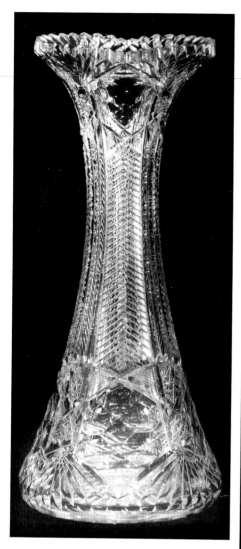

C 880. A simple but effective pattern on a vase (14 H).

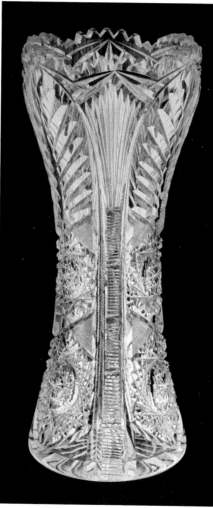

C 881. A heavily cut vase (14 H) has exceptional balance in the pattern.

C 882. A very choice vase (18 H) in a panel outline.

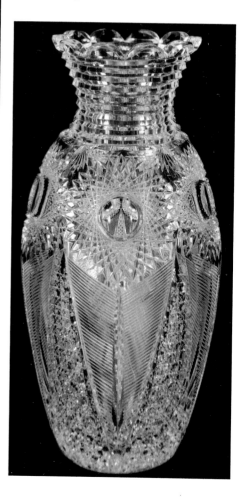

P 883. The combined pattern of panels and border on the urn (9.5 H) provides an excellent balance in pattern with shape.

P 884. The addition of handles to this vase (18 H) add value to a basic pattern.

C 886. Flashed hobstars and fan create a delicate pattern on this vase (20 H).

P 885. The double border combines with swirling panels on this vase (15 H).

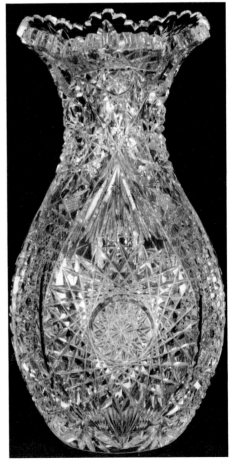

P 887. The pattern on this vase (14 H) leaves no space uncut.

C 888. The dual motifs clearly enhance the shape of this vase (10 H).

L 890. Pointed loops accent the shape of this vase (16 H).

C 891. The shape decorated with flowers on this vase (12 H) makes it noteworthy.

C 889. Heavily cut handles and a short neck make this vase (7.5 H) different.

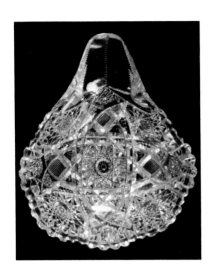

S 892. An ash tray (5.5 D), along with the thumbprint handle, adds to the limited production.

C 895. A lady's flask with a silver holder in Russian Pattern.

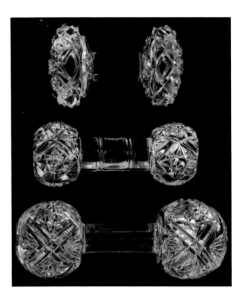

S 896, Three knife rests, the right one signed Hawkes, have detail patterns.

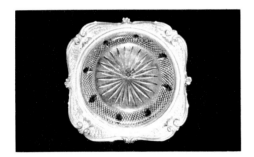

C 893. A silver rim adds to the unusual in this butter pat (3 D).

S 897. Four knife rests in unique shapes and patterns.

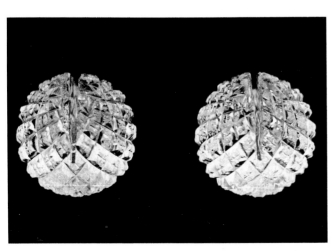

S 894. Place name holders (2 D) in Strawberry-Diamond.

S 898. A paperweight (3 D x 2 H) has a sterling silver top.

S 900. A paperweight (3.5 x 4.5)
imitates a book.

S 899. A triangular nut dish with a balanced pattern.

C 901. A string holder (4.5 D x 4.5 H) with a sterling silver lid.

CHAPTER 11 *Rarity*

Rarity in brilliant cut glass resulted from limited production. A company limited the production to only one or two pieces of a particular item. Such restrictions resulted from a number of different situations.

EXPOSITIONS

At expositions companies endeavored to alert the buyers of ornate pieces of cut glass.

1. Focal point

Generally, one company took the lead and produced an outstanding piece of cut glass as the focal point of the exhibit. Libbey, for example, exhibited the Ellsmere lamp and the extra large punch bowl. Fry centered his exhibit at one exposition around the large punch bowl in the Rochester Pattern that contained six distinct parts.

2. Exhibit Background

Companies then planned the background of the exhibit around outstanding smaller pieces. Naturally, these items needed exceptional patterns. Cut glass often centered around large trays in oval (P 902) or round shapes (P 903). Companies would possibly add an ornate vase (P 904) or a punch bowl (P 905); a heavily cut lamp (P 906) or one with a special base in the Russian Pattern (P 907).

If you look at pictures of such exhibits in published books or museums, you can recognize the shapes but not the patterns. You'll note that small and affordable items fill in the remaining spaces of the exhibit.

P 902. A tray (14 x 9.5) with an outstanding pattern.

P 903. A round tray (15 D) with a pattern good enough for exhibit at an exposition.

P 904. An ornate vase (9.5 D x 15 H) illustrates rarity.

P 905. A heavily cut punch bowl (14 D x 16 H) indicates rarity.

P 907. The foot and the Russian Pattern on this lamp make it outstanding.

P 906. The two parts and the scalloped foot suggest a lamp rarity.

L 908. A lamp (36.75 H) given to Mary Baker
Eddy.

SPECIAL ORDERS

Glass companies filled a number of special orders for cut glass.

1. Presentation

A company received a special order for a piece and asked for an engraving that gave the date, the occasion, and the name of the recipient. The person placing the order rarely asked for a known pattern. Mrs. Emilie B. Hulin presented this table lamp (L 908) to Mary Baker Eddy, founder of Christian Science.

Promoters of contests often ordered pieces as prizes. The prize, most likely, would include an acorn shaped tray (P 909) or an oval one (P 910). An urn probably caught the fancy of promoters (P 911). Lack of similar shapes supported this deduction.

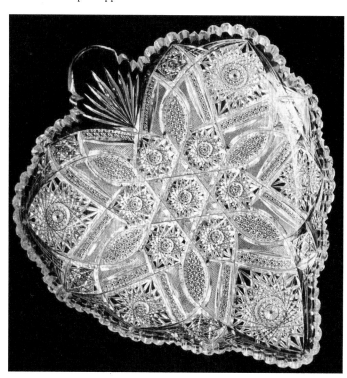

P 909. The shape and ornate
pattern of this tray qualify
it as a rarity.

P 910. The size of this oval tray in a basket weave pattern (15 x 10) rates rarity.

P 911. This urn (7 D x 12 H) blends the pattern with the shape.

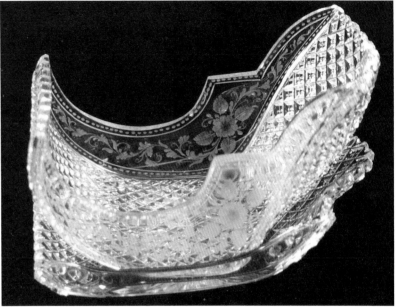

P 913. Someone placed a special order with Sinclaire for this cradle (3.5 x 7 x 4.5).

2. Gifts

Friends and relatives often placed special orders for gifts. Obviously, this wagon (P 912) and this cradle signed Sinclaire (P 913) suggest a special order.

P 912. This wagon (11.5 x 4) required a special order.

The person who ordered the gift might personalize it to the receiver as with this boxed shaving set (P 914) or this barrel wine decanter (P 915). The pattern on this decanter (P 916) contains an American flag engraved on one side and a Union Jack on the other. This lamp with the horses on the base likewise indicates a person who loved such animals (P 917).

Gifts honored birthdays or anniversaries. The giver may select a tray (P 918) or a punch bowl (P 919). When the head of a business retired, the employees donated money for an outstanding gift, such as the round tray (P 920). Usually the special gifts remained in the family and passed on to the next generation. Since these pieces appear as one of a kind, they belong in the rarity category.

P 914. This shaving mug and brush fit into a special box.

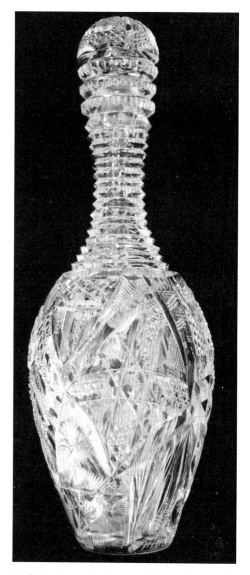

P 916. The pattern on this decanter (12 H) has an American flag on one side and the Union Jack on the other.

P 915. Someone possibly ordered this barrel in the Russian Pattern for a drinking friend.

P 917. The person who received this lamp, possibly as a gift, loved horses.

P 919. The size of this punch bowl (18 x 18) and the pattern make it exceptional.

P 918. This tray (17.5) has an excellent and expensive pattern.

P 920. The simple and balanced pattern of this tray attract attention.

P 921. This thermometer
indicates a whimsy.

Whimsies

After working hours the employees often created whimsies from the left over metal. These usually included a small but unique piece (C 921). The egg holder may or may not come under whimsy (C 922).

THE EXPERIMENTAL

Competition with other companies caused constant experimentation with new designs or additions.

1. Patterns

At times a company did a new cutting on an established pattern. This vase in Queens by Hawkes (P 923) contains an engraved flower in the alternating panels with the hobstars. A simple pattern of cobwebs certainly catches attention (P 924). As the public demanded more and more cutting on cut glass, the company may have created new patterns on large punch bowls (P 925). Use of more motifs on a large punch bowl created more of a rarity (P 926). Varying the size of the hobstars created an unusual pattern on this tray (P 927).

P 923. This vase (11 H) in Queens by Hawkes has flowers in the alternating panel.

P 922. An egg cup (4 H) may have sold singly or as part of a set.

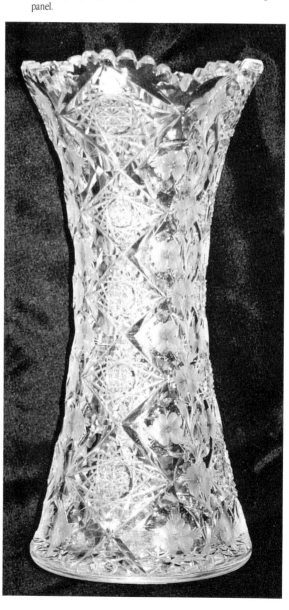

P 924. An odd pattern of a cobweb on a bowl (9 D).

P 926. The shape and size (12.5 D x 16 H) indicate this heavily cut punch bowl as a rarity.

P 925. The shape, size (14 D x 18.5 H), and the pattern make this punch bowl a rarity.

P 927. The tray size (18 x 10) and pattern place this piece in the rarity category.

P 928. The memo file (7.5) by C. F. Monroe possibly did not sell well.

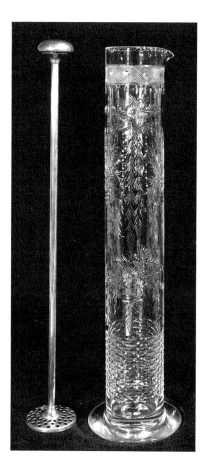

P 929. Hawkes signed this mixer for champagne and orange juice with a silver muddler.

2. Shapes

Companies began to experiment with shapes as with this letter file in Pattern #15 by Monroe (P 928) or this orange and champagne mixer with muddler signed Hawkes (P 929). Adding a shot glass to a decanter marked another effort at changing a shape (P 930). A basket twenty-one inches high (P 931) belongs in this category.

Some companies introduced a completely different shape for a standard one. A carafe (P 932) had an added square handle to match the pattern. Another company extended the lip of a jug (P 933). Hoare gave an "s-shape" to a jug in the Russian Pattern (L 934). Another company changed the shape of a punch bowl in geometric pattern (P 935) and in a floral and geometric one (P 936).

P 930. A decanter (11 H) with a shot glass as a top.

P 931. A tall basket (21 H) heavily cut.

P 932. A carafe (5.5 H) with a square handle that matches the design.

P 933. A jug with a long lip that blends with the slender body.

P 935. A punch bowl (10.5 D x 14.5 H) with a tubular bowl and a very ornate pattern.

P 934. Hoare gave an S-shape to a jug in the Russian Pattern.

P 936. A punch bowl (10.5 D x 15 H) with a tubular bowl and a grape type pattern.

3. Additions

Other companies merely added a square foot to a vase (P 937). A cone-shaped foot supported this flower center (L 938) and a ball and base became a part of the rose globe (L 939).

L 938. A flower center (10 C x 12.5 H) with a conical foot.

P 937. A vase (7 C x 11 H) with an added square foot.

L 939. A rose globe (11.5 H) in Kensington, signed Hawkes, has a ball and base added.

EXPENSIVE CREATIONS

In trying to surpass the competition, a company created expensive pieces that only a few could afford.

1. Basic Pieces

Since large trays appealed to so many, the companies focused on this shape (P 940). By comparison the average coffee pot (C 941) could not compete with the ornate one (P 942). In another comparison, a silver top on a jug raised the cost of production (C 943) but did not have the other qualities of rarity.

P 940. A large tray (9 D x 17 H) proved a costly product.

C 943. The silver and pattern on this decanter (10 H) lack the ornateness necessary for rarity.

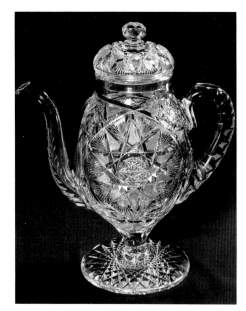

C 941. An average coffee pot (11.75 H) most companies produced provides a comparison to an expensive one.

P 942. An ornate coffee pot (12 H) with matching stopper and St. Louis Diamond neck accent the pattern to make a rarity.

2. Lamps and Candelabra

Lamps and candelabra offered the greatest opportunity to create artistry that greatly increased the asking price. To the original desk lamp, the company added hanging lights (P 944). This lamp (P 945) proved a true and costly rarity. A vase (P 946) with additional lamp fixtures few of even the wealthy could afford. Hawkes increased the number of candleholders in a candelabrum (P 947). The greatest increase in price and rarity came with this candelabrum featuring two matching candlesticks signed Hawkes in the Brazilian Pattern (L 948).

P 944. The addition of hanging globes makes this lamp rare.

P 945. A lamp (29 H) has four curved arms with prisms to hold added globes.

P 946. The company added four globes to this vase (9 H).

P 947. A candelabrum with five candleholders has a Hawkes signature.

L 948. A candelabrum with matching candle holders signed Hawkes in the Brazilian Pattern.

SILVER ARTISTRY

Companies soon recognized the effectiveness of silver on a piece of cut glass. These silver additions contained an ornate and distinctive characteristic.

1. Rims

An ornate silver rim on a bowl distinguished it from an average one (P 949). A silver rim with candleholders (P 950) indicates rarity. A celery not only has a silver rim but also four matching feet (P 951). Silver substitutes for the neck on this flower center to make it a rarity (P 952).

2. Handles

Silver with a Tiffany hallmark forms the handle on this basket to convert it to a rarity (P 953). The height of this 18.5-inch basket combines with the ornate silver handle signed Tiffany to put it in the rarity group. The silver handle and the rim obtain a rarity rating for baskets (P 954) and (P955) as well.

P 949. A bowl (13 D) contains an ornate sterling rim with a Tiffany hallmark.

P 950. This bowl (17 D) has a sterling silver rim with candleholders.

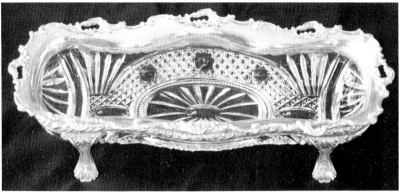

P 951. This celery (12 x 5) added a sterling silver rim and feet.

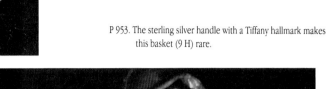

P 953. The sterling silver handle with a Tiffany hallmark makes this basket (9 H) rare.

P 952. A sterling silver top on this flower center (9 D X 11 H) provides the rarity.

P 954. The basket (18.5 H) has an ornate sterling silver handle with a Tiffany hallmark.

3. Tops

The sterling silver top by Gorham on this perfume burner assured the rarity classification (P 956). The silver on the handle, top, and foot secure a rarity category for this decanter (P 957). This piece has an even rarer top and handle (P 958). The silver shades on this pair of candelabra mark it as a rarity (P 959).

4. Signature

A signature always adds a plus when you decide on the rarity of a piece of cut glass because it identifies the source of the item. The signature of an outstanding company increases the total evaluation more than that from a lesser known company or wholesaler.

With the exception of Hawkes, these pieces have no catalog name. A "back porch" company that probably produced some of the pieces did not publish a catalog. Companies that did publish catalogs tested new pieces by placing them in a catalog as "odd" or with a number. For this entry in the catalog, they needed only one or two pieces of cut glass. If the companies received no orders for these pieces, they removed them from sale. Thus this limited the production and created a rarity.

So when you think you have found a rarity, look for the limited production, its characteristics, and proceed from there.

P 955. Adding a sterling silver handle and rim makes this basket (10 x 17) a rarity.

P 956. A perfume burner (6.5 H) with a sterling silver top by Gorham.

P 957. The sterling silver on the top, handle, foot, and overlay makes this decanter (16 H) extremely rare.

P 958. The unique sterling silver top and handle on this decanter (16 H) rate rarity.

P 959. The silver shades on the candleholders provide extras for rarity on this pair of candelabra.

CHAPTER 12 *Sharing A Collection*

You experience a special enjoyment when you share your collection with others. You not only make new friends but you often learn new facts about cut glass. You can share your collection by using it, displaying it, or photographing it.

USAGE

People who originally owned the glass used it on all occasions. You can decorate different areas of your home with cut glass.

1. Family Rooms

Most homes today have a living room used when friends visit. To save the living room from too much wear, homes include a den for the general use of the family. You can add impressively to its decor with certain pieces of cut glass. Set a basket (C 960) or a vase (C 961) on a mantle above the fireplace. In fact, a vase (C 962) or a flower center (C 963) accents the top of a bookcase, desk, or occasional table. A comport (C 964) fits spaces too small for a large vase. A nappy (C 965) with wrapped candies you can place on an occasional or coffee table. Look around these rooms for other spaces.

C 960. A basket fits easily into a space in the living areas.

C 961. Vases brighten any space.

C 962. Find a spot that can use a vase with flowers.

C 964. Comports can add beauty to smaller, bare spaces.

C 963. A flower vase improves any decor.

C 965. Put candy mints in a nappy and place it on an end or coffee table.

2. Dining Room

When you set the dining table for the family, do use your cut glass. At a place setting you can use a goblet (C 966) or a tumbler (C 967) as this one cut in Block Diamond with Star by Sandwich. Perhaps a relish (S 968) fits in along with a sugar and cream (C 969). With guests you possibly add a celery with a turned over rim (C 970) or one with a foot (C 971) that make great conversation pieces. Finally, you may serve chopped fruit from a bowl (C 972).

A number of pieces call attention to a buffet. These include a carafe with matching wines, an innovative use (C 973), a jug (C 974), or a decanter (C 975). A punch bowl (C 976) always adds interest to a buffet.

C 966. Cut glass goblets on the dining table provide a touch of beauty.

S 968. A relish dish can hold pickles or olives on the dinner table.

C 967. Any tumbler adds to a place setting especially if identified by pattern as this one in Cut Block Diamond with Star by Boston and Sandwich Glass Company.

C 969. The serving of coffee or tea needs a sugar and cream.

C 970. A celery on the dining table adapts to the serving of different foods.

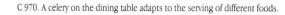

C 971. A footed celery on the dining table becomes a
conversational piece with dinner guests.

C 974. Place a jug on the buffet or on the dining table.

C 975. A jug or decanter can decorate a buffet.

C 972. A bowl functions in several ways.

C 976. A punch bowl (14 D x 15 H) becomes the focal point of
a buffet or a dining table.

C 973. Combine cut glass in different ways as with this carafe
and wines.

3. Bedroom

The dresser in a bedroom has plenty of space for pieces of cut glass. You may want to use it for a jewel (C 977) or glove (C 978) box. A puff box (C 979) or cologne always adds interest. Look at your collection and decide what pieces will fit well there, such as a dresser tray, hair receiver, a comb and brush. A lamp goes well on a bedside table.

In fact, lamps light up any spot in the home: bedroom, living areas, or hallways (L 980).

C 977. Place a jewel box (5 D) on the dresser of a guest bedroom.

C 979. Place a puff box (4 D x 4.75 H) on any dresser or chest of drawers.

C 978. A glove box (9.5 x 6 x 4) forms an artistic center on a bedroom dresser.

L 980. A long, occasional table became an excellent place to display large items.

DISPLAYING A COLLECTION

Cut glass needs displaying so you can enjoy it at all times. As you show your displays, you can share your knowledge on different items. Some collectors like to relate humorous incidents involved with the buying. Do study the individual pieces in your collection and the available space for display.

1. Antiques Cabinets

An old cabinet may have received some adaptations. Most like to replace the wooden shelves with glass ones, add a mirror to the back, and light electrically (L 981). Frequently the dealer has already made these adjustments (L 982).

Do not overlook the possibility of a corner cabinet. You may purchase an old one or have one made-to-order. With a made-to-order, the craftsman will fit the cabinet to your space.

L 981. An antiques cabinet provides a place for an elegant display of cut glass.

L 982. Mirrors, glass shelves, and lighting equipped antiques cabinets for better displays.

2. Built-in Cabinets

A number of collectors have installed open glass shelves (L 983). These do require dusting frequently to keep the glass shining. If you use Crystal Wash to clean them before placing in the open cabinet, you need to only dust them with a lambswool duster that will attract and hold dust like a magnet.

Other collectors who have the available space prefer to frame the built-in with wood and add glass (L 984). Several have endeavored to give the built-in cabinet a look of the old (L 985).

L 984. A wooden frame on a built-in cabinet gives the glass more protection.

L 985. Framing a built-in, display cabinet can give it an antique look.

L 983. Some collectors build-in open glass shelves.

3. Adaptations

Lack of space often starts the creative to work. One collector glassed in the open space under an old library table and lighted it to display large pieces (L 986). This person also collected whiskey tumblers. He found the answer in three types of cabinets: a bathroom medicine cabinet or a wall display cabinet. Shelves in an old clock case provided a means of display (L 987). For regular tumblers, he ordered an oak cabinet built to a space in the kitchen (L 988).

L 986. A collector added glass to this old-fashion, library table and used it for large pieces of cut glass.

L 987. A medicine cabinet, wall display cabinet, and an old clock case all provided display spaces for small cut glass pieces.

L 988. An oak cabinet built for a space in the kitchen to hold tumblers.

4. Glass Room

A few collectors who no longer need the space of a room in the home have used it entirely to display glass. In fact some remodeled and added a room for glass display. In this glass room the cabinets cover the walls completely (L 989) and (L 990). The collector could use large pieces or small pieces only or intermingle the two.

So study your collection and your space. Try to find unique ways to display your collection at all times.

L 989. A view of one corner of a glass room.

L 990. Another view of a glass room.

PHOTOGRAPHING YOUR GLASS

Anyone can learn to take good photographs of glass with some basic instructions. We can simply explain the method we used.

1. Photo Table

We constructed this table so that we could easily take it apart and put it in the trunk of the car. If you have the space, you need not make it collapsible. To fold away for traveling, we used right angle aluminum for the frame. With a stationary one, use wood for the frame. You will need the following parts for wood or aluminum:

> **4 pieces of 66 inches**
> **4 pieces of 24 inches to form the top of the table and join the tall poles**
> **4 hard plastic pieces 24 x 12 inches**
> **2 frosted plastic pieces 24 x 28 inches**
> **1 piece of frosted plastic 24 x 66 inches**

Directions: Measure 42 inches from the ground on the tall poles. At this point join the tall poles with the 24-inch ones to form the frame. Place the large piece of plastic from the top of the tall poles to the front edge of the frame for a curved background. Place one bracer at the front of the table along the front edge of the curved plastic. Measure six inches from the floor and place other bracers on the three sides. Drill holes for screws and bolts to fit the collapsible frame together. Used pointed screws on the wooden one.

If you want a white background, you do not need the frosty plastic sides. Take colored pieces against the white background. With a black background, anchor the frosted plastic sides to the front poles. Cover the curved frosty plastic with black felt. Depending on the thickness, you may need double or triple pieces of felt measuring 24 x 66 inches for deep black (L 991).

2. Equipment

Most of you already own a camera. You will need a tripod to hold the camera steady. Most pictures require at least two flood lights and stands. We found using a third flood to bounce light off the ceiling improved the sharpness of the pictures.

With a black background you place the flood lights usually at an angle on either side. For the white background place the flood lights at the back and underneath the table. Use the viewer on the camera to find the best position for the flood lights. We did not use a flash as we found it resulted in scattered bright spots on the picture.

You will need several sizes of plastic holders from large to small, depending on the different sizes you plan to photograph. We like to use the clear plastic ones as they don't detract from the piece. Secure a piece of clear plastic about two inches in length and about a half inch in thickness. You can insert this under the front of a piece or under the back for a sharper focus.

Focus

Always trust the focus of your camera when you look through the viewer. Keep moving the tripod in or out until the "X" covers the center of the piece. Adjust your flood lights to equalize the light from all sides on the piece. You will get in the picture what you see through the viewer of the camera.

Determine the best angle from which to take the piece of cut glass by studying old catalogs or pictures in our previous books. These will suggest the best position to show the entire pattern clearly on the shape. For flat pieces you find little difficulty with the focus.

Focusing on curved or round pieces present a real problem. Try to place the piece so that you see the minor and major motifs clearly. With major motifs, as a hobstar or pinwheel, take only a part for recognition and focus on the minor ones that provide most of the identification. By raising the back or front may give you a clearer focus. This raising particularly improves the focus with footed pieces. Handles show clearer by slightly turning them to one side. If you can not get a good focus on a sugar and cream, take the bottom of one and the profile of the other. You may want to take the sugar and the cream separatley and then put the two together.

Always center the piece, leaving a fairly equal border on all sides. Make sure you do not cut off part of the shape. Use black and white film with crystal pieces. The colored film will dull the picture of a crystal piece. Always remember the reader wants to see the pattern clearly for matching.

L 991. A photographic table.

If you or a friend develop your pictures, you can custom print them. You can give any bright spot a little more light to even the picture. When you have them commercially developed and they come out too light, you ask for a darker print of the negative.

4. Uses for Pictures

You will find a number of uses for your photographs. Most of you keep a card file on th pieces in your collection. You can add a picture to the information card. If you fail to describe the piece so anyone would recognize it, as an insurance adjuster, the picture will do the job.

You may want to send friends or relatives a picture of your latest purchase. If you update a collection, you will need pictures for advertising. A number of collectors have placed the pictures in an album and take it to the national convention or to a chapter meeting. From time to time, you will substitute other pictures in the album to expand interest.

To go along with the album, a number of collectors have recorded an audio cassette. The cassette makes the album complete. A few collectors have rented a video camera and made a video cassette of their collection for an insurance record. You can focus on one piece at a time, calling attention to the shape, the size, the pattern, or any other pertinent information. If you visit a fellow collector, take along the video tape. It offers the perfect way to share a collection.

BUILDING RECOGNITION

The American Cut Glass Association and its chapters have accomplished a great deal in winning outstanding recognition for brilliant cut glass. Where someone use to say, "I can't believe the Americans produced the finest brilliant cut glass," now many say instead, "Did you know that for forty years the Americans created the most beautiful brilliant cut glass in the world?" This recognition has resulted from outstanding displays of brilliant cut glass.

1. Museums

Chapter members have loaned local museums cut glass from their collections for a display of American brilliant cut glass. A museum in San Francisco agreed to do a display for three weeks. The exhibit proved so popular that the museum extended the time to four months. Even a museum in England decided to display American cut glass.

2. Local Libraries

Libraries have available display cabinets. Collectors and members of ACGA have loaned glass for an exhibit, and some members have volunteered to give lectures.

3. Colleges and Universities

These educational institutions have taken an interest in cut glass. One in Texas has displayed cut glass that members of the American Cut Glass Association have loaned the college.

4. Clubs

Both antiques and women's clubs seek speakers for programs. American cut glass has become a very popular subject. Women bring in their glass for identification.

5. Antiques Shows

Those who put on antiques shows have found that lectures by experts bring in a crowd. Several have featured lectures on American brilliant cut glass.

As you can see, sharing information on American cut glass continues to spread. So take great pride in your collection when you show and tell about it, for you own the finest brilliant cut glass ever produced.

Appendix

Signatures/Marks

C.G. ALFORD & COMPANY
New York, New York

BUFFALO CUT GLASS COMPANY
Batavia, New York

ALMY & THOMAS
Corning, New York

T.B. CLARK & COMPANY
Honesdale, Pennsylvania

AMERICAN WHOLESALE CORP.
Baltimore, Maryland

CORONA CUT GLASS COMPANY
Toledo, Ohio

M.J. AVERBECK MANUFACTURER
New York, New York

C. DORFLINGER & SONS
White Mills, Pennsylvania

J.D. BERGEN COMPANY
Meriden, Connecticut

O.F. EGGINTON COMPANY
Corning, New York

H.C. FRY GLASS COMPANY
Rochester, Pennsylvania

HOBBS, BROCKUNIER & COMPANY
Wheeling, West Virginia

HAWKES

T.G. HAWKES & COMPANY
Corning, New York

HOPE GLASS WORKS
Providence, Rhode Island

L. HINSBERGER CUT GLASS COMPANY
New York, New York

HUNT GLASS COMPANY
Corning, New York

HOARE

J. HOARE & COMPANY
Corning, New York

IORIO GLASS SHOP
Flemington, New Jersey

HOBBS GLASS COMPANY
Wheeling, West Virginia

IRVING CUT GLASS COMPANY
Honesdale, Pennsylvania

LAUREL CUT GLASS COMPANY
Jermyn, Pennsylvania

LACKAWANNA CUT GLASS COMPANY
Scranton, Pennsylvania

LIBBEY GLASS COMPANY
Toledo, Ohio

LYONS CUT GLASS COMPANY
Lyons, New York

MAJESTIC CUT GLASS COMPANY
Elmira, New York

MAPLE CITY GLASS COMPANY
Hawley, Pennsylvania

MC KANNA CUT GLASS COMPANY
Honesdale, Pennsylvania

LOWELL CUT GLASS CO.
LOWELL MASS

LOWELL CUT GLASS COMPANY
Lowell, Massachusetts

C.F. M.C^{o}

C. F. MONROE COMPANY
Meriden, Connecticut

NEWARK CUT GLASS COMPANY
Newark, New Jersey

PAIRPOINT CORPORATION
New Bedford, Massachusetts

F. X. PARSCHE & SON COMPANY
Chicago, Illinois

PITKIN & BROOKS
Chicago, Illinois

SENECA GLASS COMPANY
Morgantown, West Virginia

SIGNET GLASS COMPANY
Corning, New York

H. P. SINCLAIRE & COMPANY
Corning, New York

STERLING GLASS COMPANY
Cincinnati, Ohio

L. STRAUS & SONS
New York, New York

TAYLOR BROTHERS
Philadelphia, Pennsylvania

TUTHILL CUT GLASS COMPANY
Middletown, New York

VAN HEUSEN CHARLES COMPANY
Albany, New York

UNGER BROTHERS
Newark, New Jersey

WRIGHT RICH CUT GLASS COMPAN
Anderson, Indiana

CANADIAN CUT GLASS SIGNATURES

HOUSE OF BIRKS
Montreal, Canada

GUNDY, CLAPPERTON COMPANY
Toronto, Canada

RODEN BROTHERS, LTD.
Toronto, Canada

GOWANS, KENT & COMPANY LIMITED
Toronto, Canada

**NATIONAL ASSOCIATION OF
CUT GLASS MANUFACTURERS
IN UNITED STATES AND CANADA**

Broeker Mitchell

 ASH BROS. OM^{E}G^{A}

  ELLIS

 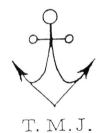 

T. M. J.

 DIAMOND C H

Bibliography

Avila, George C. *The Pairpoint Glass Story.* New Bedford, MA: Reynolds DeWalt Printing, Inc., 1968.

Barlow, Raymond E. & Joan E. Kaiser. *A Guide to Sandwich Glass.* Windham NH: Barlow-Kaiser Publishing Company, Inc., 1987.

Boggess, Bill and Louise. *American Brilliant Cut Glass.* New York: Crown Publishers, Inc., 1977.

_____. *Collecting American Brilliant Cut Glass.* Atglen, PA: Schiffer Publishing Ltd., 1992.

_____. *Identifying American Brilliant Cut Glass.* New York: Crown Publishers, Inc., 1984.

_____. *Identifying American Brilliant Cut Glass.* Atglen, PA: Schiffer Publishing Ltd., 1991. Revised and enlarged edition with value guide.

Collector's Illustrated Price Guide to Cut Glass. Paducah, KY: Collectors Books, 1977.

Daniel, Dorothy. *Cut and Engraved Glass 1771-1905.* New York: M. Barrows & Company, Inc., 1950.

_____. *Price Guide to American Cut Glass.* New York: William Morrow & Company, Inc., 1967.

DiBartolomeo, Robert E. *American Glass.* Princeton, NJ: Pyne Press, 1974.

Ehrhardt, Alpha. *Cut Glass Price Guide.* Kansas City: Heart of America Press, 1973 (contains 8 catalogs).

Evers, Jo. *The Standard Cut Glass Value Guide.* Paducah, KY: Collectors Books, 1975 (contains 5 catalogs).

Farrar, Estelle Sinclaire. *H.P. Sinclaire, Jr. Glass Maker. v. 1.* Garden City, NY: Farrar Books, 1974 (contains inventory photographs).

Farrar, Estelle Sinclaire and Jane Spillman. *The Complete Cut and Engraved Glass of Corning.* New York: Crown Publishers, Inc., 1979 (contains inventory pictures of Sinclaire glass).

Fauster, Carl U. *Libbey Glass.* Toledo, OH: Len Beach Press, 1979.

Feller, John Quentin. *Dorflinger America's Finest Glass, 1852-1921.* Marieta, OH: Antique Publications, 1988.

Fry Glass Club. *Encyclopedia of Fry Glass.* Paducah, KY: Collectors Books, 1989.

Gillander, William. *Treatise on Art of Glassmaking.* 1854. Second Edition.

Glass Container Manufacturers Institute. *Billions of Bottles.* New York, 1959.

Hodkin, F.W. and A. Cousen. *A Text Book of Glass Technology.* New York: D. Van Nostrand Company, 1925.

Hotchkiss, John F. *Cut Glass Handbook and Price Guide.* Des Moines, IA: Wallace-Homestead Book Company, 1970.

Kovel, Ralph M. and Terry H. *A Directory of American Silver, Pewter and Silver Plate.* New York: Crown Publishers, Inc., 1961.

Libbey Glass, 1818-1968. Toledo, OH: Toledo Museum of Art, 1968.

Lightner Museum. *American Brilliant Cut Glass, Masterpieces from Lightner Museum.* St. Augustine, FL, 1991.

McKearin, Helen and George S. *American Glass.* New York: Crown Publishers, Inc., 1946.

Mebane, John. *Collecting Bride Baskets.* Des Moines, IA: Wallace-Homestead Book Company, 1976.

Newman, Harold. *An Illustrated Dictionary of Glass.* London: Thames Publishing Company, 1977.

Oliver, Elizabeth. *American Antique Glass.* New York: Golden Press, 1977.

Padgett, Leonard. *Pairpoint Glass.* Des Moines, IA: Wallace-Homestead Book Company, 1979.

Pearson, J. Michael. *Encyclopedia of American Cut and Engraved Glass.* 3 volumes. Miami Beach, FL, 1975-1977.

_____. *Adventures and Mis-Adventures of Antique Dealers and Collectors.* 1993.

Pearson, J. Michael and Dorothy T. *American Cut Glass for Discriminating Collectors.* New York, 1965.

_____. *American Cut Glass Collections.* Miami Beach, FL, 1969.

Pennsylvania Glassware, 1870-1904. Princeton: The Pryne Press, 1972.

Phillips, David Brandon. *Objects of American Brilliant Period Cut and Engraved Glass, 1880-1910.* 1985.

Rainwater, Dorothy T. *Encyclopedia of American Silver Manufacturers.* West Chester, PA: Schiffer Publishing, Ltd., 1986.

Revi, Albert Christian. *American Cut and Engraved Glass.* New York: Thomas Nelson & Sons, 1965.

_____. *The Spinning Wheel's Complete Book of Antiques.* New York: Grosset & Dunlap, 1972.

Schroeder, Bill. *Cut Glass.* Paducah, KY: Collectors Books, 1977.

Spillman, Jane Shadel. *Glass Tableware and Vases.* New York: Alfred A. Knopf, Inc., 1982.

_____. *White House Glassware.* The White House Historical Association, 1989.

Stevens, George. *Canadian Glass, 1825-1925.* Toronto: Ryerson Press, 1967.

Swan, Martha Louise. *American Cut and Engraved Glass of the Brilliant Period.* Lonbard, IL: Wallace-Homestead Book Company, 1986.

Victoria and Albert Museum. *Glass Table-Ware.* 1947.

Waher, Bettye W. *The Hawkes Hunter, 1880-1962.* 1984.

Warman, Edwin G. *American Cut Glass.* Uniontown, PA: E.G. Warman Publishing, Inc., 1954.

Weiner, Herbert and Freda Lipkowitz. *Rarities in American Cut Glass.* Houston, TX: Collectors House of Books Publishing Company, 1975.

Wilson, Kenneth M. *Glass in New England.* Old Stourbridge Meriden, CT, 1969.

Catalogs

Alford Cut Glass, 1904.

Ben Allen & Company, 1924.

American Cut Glass Association Reprints:
    Dorflinger: Line Drawings.
    T.G. Hawkes & Company.
    J. Hoare and Company.
    Maple City Glass Company and T.B. Clark & Company.
    Meriden Cut Glass Company-Wilcox Silver Plate Company.

Averheck Rich Cut Glass: catalog #104, undated.

Baracat Catalolgue.

Bergen Cut Glass Company: 1904-1905, 1907-1908, 2 undated.

Blackmer Cut Glass: 1904, 1906-1907.

Buffalo Cut Glass Company catalog.

T.B. Clark & Company: 1896, 1901, undated, 1905, 1908, undated.

Covington Cut Glass Company, 1915.

C. Dorflinger & Sons: catalog #51, 1881-1921, undated.

_____: catalog Kalana Art Glass.

O.F. Egginton Company catalog.

Elmira Cut Glass Company catalog.

Empire Cut Glass Company: 1906, 1910, 1912.

H.C. Fry Glass Company catalog.

Gundy-Clapperton Company: 1909, 1915.

T.G. Hawkes & Company: American Cut Glass Association catalog, 14 catalogs of Brilliant Period, two late catalogs, and advertising booklet, undated.

Higgins & Seiter: 1893, 1899, #7, #17, #19.

J. Hoare & Company: three catalogs with no dates, 1911 catalog, and undated scrapbook.

G.W. Huntley, 1913.

Irving Cut Glass Company, Inc. catalog.

Keystone Cut Glass Company catalog.

Kranz & Smith Company catalog.

Lackawanna Cut Glass Company: two catalogs.

Laurel Cut Glass Company: two catalogs; one 1907, other undated.

Libbey Glass Company: 1893, 1896, 1898, 1904, 1905, 1908, 1909, 1900-1910, c. 1920, 2 undated.

Liberty Cut Glass Works catalog.

Linford Cut Glass Company catalog.

Lotus Cut Glass Company: No. 49, No. 50.

Luzerne Cut Glass Company: two catalogs with no dates.

Maple City Glass Company: 1904 #3, 1906 #5, 1911 #10.

Marshall Field, 1896.

Meriden Cut Glass Company catalog.

C.F. Monroe Company catalog #6, other undated.

Mt. Washington Glass Works: 5 catalogs of Brilliant Period.

Niagara Cut Glass Company: two catalogs.

Ottawa Cut Glass Company, 1913.

Pairpoint Corporation: American Cut Glass Association catalog and 5 undated catalogs.

Pairpoint Manufacturing Company Gold and Silver Plate, 1894.

Parcel Post Cut Glass Company catalog.

F.X. Parsche & Sons catalog.

Phillips Cut Glass Company catalog.

Phoenix Glass Company: 1893 and one undated.

Pitkin & Brooks: 1907 and 3 undated.

Powelton Cut Glass Company catalog.

Quaker City Cut Glass Company: two catalogs undated.

Rochester Cut Glass Company catalog.

Roden Brothers, 1917.

Silver Plate and Sterling Silver Catalogue of 1888 by W.G. Crook.

Sinclaire Sketches and Office Corresponces Papers.

Steuben Glass Works catalog.

L. Straus & Sons, 1893.

Taylor Brothers: two catalogs.

F.B. Tinker, 2 undated catalogs.

Tuthill Cut Glass Company, The Connoisseur.

Unger Brothers: two catalogs: 1906 and one undated.

Unidentified Salesman's Catalogue, 1890-1905.

Unidentified catalog, possibly Hoare.

Val Saint-Lambert, 1906, 1908.

Wallenstein Mayer Company, 1913.

Waterford Glass Company, undated.

Wilcox Silver Plate Company, undated.

Index of Identified Patterns

PATTERN NUMBER	COMPANY	ILLUSTRATION
Acme	Averbeck	S 411
Adonis	Clark	C 452
Albert	Empire	C 479
Alexis	Fry	S 491
Alsatia	Maple City	S 617
Amaranth	Laurel	C 587
American	Fry	C 492
American Beauty	Clark	C 447
Anemone	Clark	C 443
Angelus	Pairpoint	C 649
Antique No. 1 & Engr.	Sinclaire	C 682
Antoinette	Straus	S 707
Arcadia	Sterling	C 702
Argo	Hawkes	C 509
Ariel	Monroe	P 634
Aster	Bergen	S 425
Aster	Roden	C 734
Aster	Sinclaire	C 696
Asteroid	Fry	S 488
Aurora Borealis	P & B	C 668
Avilla	Pairpoint	C 363
Baronial	Sinclaire	S 372
Bedford	Mt. Washington	C 642
Bellmere	Monroe	C 635
Belmont	Dorflinger	C 466
Belmont	P & B	C 366
Berkshire	Egginton	S 473
Berwick	Pairpoint	C 651
Blackberry	Tuthill	C 725
Block	Dorflinger	S 117
Block Diamond	Mt. Washington	S 117
Block Diamond with Star	Sandwich	C 967
Border	P & B	S 364
Boston	Averbeck	S 294
Brazilian	Hawkes	L 948
Brilliant	Pairpoint	C 650
Brilliante	Dorflinger	C 75
Buffalo	Sinclaire	S 685
Burton	Maple City	A 618
Byrns	P & B	C 671
Cactus	Pairpoint	S 652
Cairo	Hoare	S 548
Calve	Egginton	P 310
Canna	Clark	C 453
Canton	Averbeck	S 412
Cardinal	Hawkes	C 314
Cardinal	Maple City	S 611
Carnation	Fry	S 485
Carnival	Egginton	C 474
Carot	Clark	C 454
Cassia	Bergen	S 417
Celtic	Blackmer	C 428
Cleo	P & B	S 367
Columbia	Quaker City	C 679
Constellation	Sinclaire	P 686
Corncel	Hoare	S 326
Cornell	Taylor Bros.	C 717
Cornwall	Sinclaire	P 683
Corona	Blackmer	C 434
Coronation	Gundy Clapperton	C 398
Corsican	Maple City	C 613
Crescent	Laurel	C 589
Crete	Hawkes	S 499
Crystal City	Hoare	P 549
Cypress	Laurel	S 588
Daisy	Pairpoint	C 661
Dallas	Bergen	C 298
Dauphin	Pairpoint	C 653
Dawson	Taylor Bros.	C 718
Deer	Sinclaire	P 701
Delhi	Hawkes	C 510
Delphic	Maple City	S 615
Delphos	Libbey	C 341
Deray	Libbey	S 619
Desdemona	Clark	S 445
Devonshire	Hawkes	S 500
Devonshire	Maple City	C 356
Diamond & Silver Thread	Sinclaire	C 60, C 684
Dolphin	Maple City	C 620
Dora	Bergen	P 418
Dorian	Maple City	S 610
Duberry	Quaker City	C 680
Ducal	Straus	S 705
Duchess	Pairpoint	S 654
Dupont	Allen	C 406
Dutch	Pairpoint	S 647
Elaine	Bergen	C 299
Elba	Fry	C 486
Elba	Hawkes	C 511
Eleanor	Hoare	C 550
Electra	Pairpoint	S 655
Electra	Strauss	C 704
Elk	Irving	C 580
El Tova	Clark	P 451
Empress	P & B	C 670
Empress	Quaker City	P 371
Engadine	Dorflinger	C 469
Engraved Roses	Sinclaire	S 697
Essen	Lackawanna	S 585
Estelle	Blackmer	S 432
Eudora	Blackmer	S 435
Excelsior	Bergen	P 416
Florentine	Clark	S 455
Florodora	Unger	S 727
Flute	Clark	S 448
Flute & Greek Key	Hawkes	S 505
Flute & Miter	Libbey	C 592
Freedom	Fry	C 493
Fuchia	Sinclaire	S 693
Genoa	Averbeck	C 293
Glencoe	Hawkes	C 315
Glenda	Libbey	C 339
Georgia	Higgins & Seiter	C 738
Globe	Bergen	S 419
Grapes	Tuthill	C 388
Graphic Cosmo	Hawkes	S 542
Harmony	Hawkes	P 501
Harvard	Hoare	P 544
Harvard	Libbey	S 97
Harvest	Clark	S 456
Heart	Fry	S 494
Hebron	Maple City	S 614
Hob Diamond	Dorflinger	C 119
Idaho	Sinclaire	P 687
Imperial	Pairpoint	S 656
Inverness	Dorflinger	P 309
Iola	Blackmer	S 436
Ionian	Clark	P 449
Iowa	Irving	S 335
Iredel	Lackawanna	C 583
Iroquois	Egginton	C 475
Ivy	Bergen	C 415
Jersey	Hawkes	C 512
Jet	Bergen	S 740
Jewel	Libbey	C 342
Jewel	Clark	C 442
Juno	Hawkes	S 502
Kensington	Hawkes	L 939
Keystone	Fry	C 487
Keystone	P & B	C 672
King George	P & B	S 667
Kingston	Libbey	C 338
Lafayette	Sinclaire	S 690
Lakefield	Lakefield	S 402
Libbey	Libbey	C 355
Liberty	Averbeck	C 295
Lista	Maple City	C 357
Logan	Bergen	S 300
Lotus	Allen	S 407
Lustre	P & B	C 673
Madame	Empress	C 477
Marbella	Clark	S 450
Marigold	Pairpoint	C 657
Marlo	Blackmer	S 437
Mathilda	Libbey	C 594
Mavis	Pairpoint	C 658
Medina	Blackmer	P 429
Memphis	P & B	C 290
Meteor	Pairpoint	S 659
Minerva	Hawkes	S 506
Mona	Hawkes	C 507
Monarch	Hoare	C 551

Name	Company	Illustration
Morgan	Libbey	S 354
Myrtle	P & B	S 368
Nakada	Monroe	C 636
Naples	Averbeck	P 413
Naples	Hoare	C 129, C 552
Narada	Monroe	C 631
Nashville	Fry	S 489
Nassau	Hoare	S 327
Nassau	Libbey	C 591
Nevada	Monroe	S 631
Newport	Clark	C 441
Nordel	Blackmer	P 433
Norma	Straus	C 703
Norway	Huntley	S 740
Norwood	Hawkes	S 503
Oakland	Lackawanna	C 586
Oakland	Roden	C 735
Old Colony	Dorflinger	C 471
Old Irish	Meriden	P 629
Onica	Maple City	S 621
Oregon	Blackmer	C 438
Oxford	Hawkes	S 513
Oxia	Maple City	S 612
Persian	Hawkes or Hoare	C 81
Petrel	Maple City	P 622
Pheasant	Hawkes	C 539
Pheasant	Sinclaire	P 700
Pilgram	Hawkes	S 514
Plaza	Empire	C 481
Plymouth	Meriden	C 360
Plymouth	P & B	C 365
Pontiac	Clark	C 446
Poppy	Tuthill	C 53, P 57
Pricilla	Mt. Washington	S 645
Prima Donna	Clark	C 258
Prince	P & B	C 666
Princess	Libbey	C 343
Princess	O'Connor	S 361
Prism	Averbeck	S 292
Prism	Bergen	S 106, S 297
Prism	Hoare	S 546
Prism	Monroe	C 632
Prism	P & B	C 669
Queens	Sinclaire	C 373
Rajah	Libbey	C 344
Rajah	P & B	S 369
Reaper	Clark	S 457
Regina	Roden	C 736
Renaissance	Dorflinger	S 69
Renton	Empire	C 480
Renwich	Bergen	P 420
Rex	Straus	S 706
Richmond	Blackmer	C 439
Roman	Egginton	C 476
Romano	Libbey	C 593
Royal	Roden	S 733
Russian	Dorflinter	C 70, C 72, C 75
Russian	Fry	S 84
Russian	Hawkes	C 68, C 71, C 73, C 76, C 77, C 79, C 89
Russian	Hoare	C 87, C 88
Russian or Pattern #60	Washington	C 638, L 934
Russian	New England	C 74
Russian and Fan	Hoare	C 80
San Marcos	Clark	S 302
Satin Iris	Hawkes	S 324
Savoy	Pairpoint	S 648
Seneca	Lackawanna	S 584
Seward	Maple City	C 616
Sheldon	Bergen	C 421
Sillsbee	Pairpoint	C 662
Silver Thread	Libbey	C 345
Sparkler	Hoare	S 553
Spokane	Fry	S 490
Spruce	Averbeck	S 296
Star	P & B	C 674
Star and Feather	Libbey	C 340
Stars, Hollows & Engr.	Sinclaire	C 695
Stratford	Clark	C 444
Stratford	Huntley	C 739
Stratford	Sinclaire	C 691
Sultana	Blackmer	C 430
Sunburst	Fry	S 495
Sunburst	Parsche	C 664
Table Diamond	Hawkes	P 504
Tasso	Hoare	S 547
Texal	Maple City	S 623
Three Fruits	Hawkes	P 323
Three Cut Octagon	Mt. Washington	C 640
Two Cut Octagon	Mt. Washington	C 644
Tiger Lily	Tuthill	C 724
Triton	Blackmer	C 440
Tyroee	Bergen	P 422
Urn & Flame	Pairpoint	C 660
Viceroy	Bergen	C 423
Victrola	Irving	S 334
Vienna	Averbeck	C 114
Viola	Empire	C 478
Wabash	Bergen	C 301
Wallace	Quaker City	S 681
Weldon	Maple City	S 358
Winola	Clark	C 458
Winona	P & B	C 675
Westminister	Mt. Washington	C 643
Wheat	Hoare	C 88
X-ray	Libbey	C 595
York	Hoare	S 554
Yucatan	Hoare	C 555

PATTERN NUMBER	COMPANY	ILLUSTRATION
#1	Elmira	S 482
#2	Hawkes	S 515
#3	Hawkes	S 516
#15	Monroe	P 928
#16	Blackmer	C 431
#21	Elmira	C 483
#30	Libbey	S 596
#36	Libbey	S 597
#39	Elmira	S 484
#39	Libbey	S 598
#40	Sinclaire	C 694
#80	Dorflinger	S 308
#120	Libbey	S 599
#125	Meriden	S 628
#136	Libbey	C 512
#210	Dorflinger	S 467
#226F	Meriden	C 359
#231F	Meriden	S 627
#307	Roden	C 737
#647	P & B	C 676
#682	Dorflinger	C 468
#1422	Hawkes	C 508
#1531	Hoare	C 558
#1554	Hoare	S 557
#1650	Meridan	C 630
#1920	Sinclaire	S 291
#3708	Hawkes	C 116
#5401	Hoare	S 325
#8677	Hoare	S 556
#9546	Hoare	C 559
#9595	Hoare	C 560
#9922	Hoare	S 561
#70130	Marshall Field	C 741
#70426	Marshall Field	P 742
#71524	Marshall Field	S 743
#76003	Marshall Field	S 744

PATENT NUMBER	COMPANY	ILLUSTRATION
#19,865	Hawkes	S 498
#22,663	Hibbler	S 543
#23,317	Bergen	S 426
#27,060	American	P 410
#27,061	American	C 409
#27,062	American	C 408
#36,866	Ohio	C 362
#38,001	Libbey	C 353
#44,421	Kupfer	S 337
9/22/91	Bergen	P 427

Index of Colored Cut Glass Patterns

Index of Companies

Values Guide

We, the authors of this book, greatly emphasize that a value guide contains only a basic range of prices that requires adjustment to such factors as: geographical area, condition of the item, signature, rarity--to name only a few. Neither the authors nor the publisher assume any responsibility for any loss that occurs by using this value guide.

	Standard	Choice	Premium
BASKETS			
Bonbon	150-295	300-425	425-575
Flower 16"	600-850	1200-1500	1800-2200
BELL			
Small 4"-5"	125-175	175-275	275-450
Large 6"-7"	200-275	275-400	400-550
BONBON			
Handled 5"	60-100	100-175	200-275
Covered 6"	125-175	175-250	250-450
Footed 5"-6"	175-225	225-300	325-525
BOTTLES			
Bitters w/Top	150-200	200-275	275-300
Cologne 6"	275-350	375-475	500-950
Ketchup	100-175	250-325	325-475
Perfume 5"-6"	175-250	275-375	400-650
BOWLS			
Finger	75-100	150-300	325-450
Berry 8"	150-225	350-850	1000-3500
Low 10"	200-275	350-850	900-3500
Divided 9"	175-300	350-500	600-1200
Handled/Footed	175-300	350-500	600-1200
Orange 10"	175-225	250-400	450-1250
Whipped Cream 6"-7"	125-225	250-400	425-700
BOXES			
Glove	600-750	800-1400	1500-3500
Handkerchief	425-500	500-850	850-2000
Puff/Hair	75-125	150-250	275-450
Jewel (round)	475-600	600-900	900-2650
BUTTER			
Covered	300-475	500-750	750-1400
Pat	25-40	50-75	90-125
Tub	150-225	250-400	450-700
Stick/Fluff	100-175	225-400	550-900
CANDLESTICK			
Single 10"	150-225	250-325	350-600
Pair	375-550	900-1200	1400-2200
Candelabrum (single)	900-1200	1400-1750	1800-3700
CARAFES			
Regular	60-125	125-250	275-450
Night Cap	225-400	425-650	700-1000
CELERY			
Oval	75-175	200-325	350-600
Footed	n/a	950-1400	1450-2250
Upright	200-325	350-475	600-825
CHEESE			
Covered	175-275	325-600	650-1000
Cheese & Cracker	150-225	250-375	400-650
COMPOTES			
Squat	90-325	200-325	375-600
Tall 10"-12"	250-375	500-950	1000-2200
Covered	250-375	400-800	800-1700
Handled	175-250	275-575	750-1000
Divided	175-250	275-575	750-1000
DECANTERS			
Wine	350-900	1200-1500	1850-4250
Whiskey 12'	350-600	900-1600	1800-3800

	Standard	Choice	Premium
Handled	475-900	1300-1800	1800-4000
Demijohn	650-975	1000-1500	1500-3500
Tantalus (2 bottle)	1000-1500	1500-2500	2500-4500
DISH			
Oval/Round 5"	75-175	200-425	450-1000
Square 8"-9"	450-850	900-1350	1400-2600
Covered dish	n/a	1250-2000	2000-3800
Handled	150-275	275-400	400-900
FLOWER HOLDER			
Center 10"	750-1000	1100-1600	1800-2800
Globe 7"	225-375	400-700	700-1400
Canoe 12"	550-800	800-1100	1200-1800
Ferner 8"	125-200	225-375	400-750
Violet	100-125	150-225	250-425
Footed Bowl	275-400	425-675	700-1000
Pot 6"	175-250	275-350	400-700
GLASSWARE			
Champagne	25-50	50-100	150-350
Claret	25-40	50-75	100-300
Wine	25-35	45-70	100-300
Cordial	20-30	40-60	70-100
Tumbler	20-30	50-100	100-350
Shot	20-35	45-70	85-400
Ale	40-80	90-150	150-350
Sherry	25-35	45-70	100-250
Mug	150-200	225-400	400-750
ICE			
Bowl	225-425	450-650	650-975
Tub	200-350	375-600	625-900
JARS			
Cracker	650-1000	1050-1600	1800-3600
Tobacco 7"	800-1200	1400-2400	2500-4000
Cigar 8"	850-1300	1500-2500	2600-4250
JUG			
Champagne	550-775	800-1400	1500-3200
Tankard	475-625	650-1250	1300-2200
Footed	500-675	700-1350	1400-2400
Lemonade	425-550	575-825	850-1400
Bulbous	625-775	800-1300	1400-2000
Silver Trim	725-900	1000-1600	1700-4800
LAMPS			
Oil 7"-8"	800-1100	1200-1800	1900-2600
Small	2000-3500	4000-6500	7000-12000
Tall	4500-6500	6500-9500	9500-27000
MISCELLANEOUS			
Loving Cup (small)	n/a	275-475	n/a
Loving Cup (large)	475-600	650-800	900-1200
Clock 5"-6"	400-500	525-650	675-900
Flask 4"	135-160	175-250	275-425
String Box	n/a	325-475	n/a
Muscilage	n/a	225-500	n/a
Paperweight	n/a	325-550	n/a
Toothpick	30-60	75-150	200-1500
NAPPIES			
No Handle 6"	50-80	80-150	200-700
One Handle 6"	60-85	100-175	225-750

Item			
Two Handle 7 "	85-125	150-225	275-900
Three Handle 5"-6"	125-165	200-275	325-950
OILS			
Small	125-175	190-275	300-575
Tall	150-190	200-375	400-775
Footed	225-300	350-850	900-2400
PICKLE/RELISH			
Scenic 8"	275-350	375-475	500-800
Handled	75-125	150-350	375-575
Oval	60-90	125-275	300-650
PLATES			
5"-6"	90-150	175-250	300-750
7"-8"	100-175	200-375	400-2200
9"-10"	200-275	300-400	400-2200
POTS			
Tea	1600-1800	1800-2500	2500-5500
Coffee	2500-3200	3200-5000	5000-8500
PUNCH BOWLS			
One Piece 14"	750-1500	1500-2200	2200-4500
Two Piece Tall 14"	1100-2000	2000-3500	3500-6000
Two Piece Squat 12"	1000-1500	1500-2500	2500-5000
Two Piece Small12"-14"	1000-1400	1400-2500	2500-5500
Two Piece Large15"-18"	1400-2200	2300-3800	3800-8000
SAUCERS			
Round 5"	60-90	100-225	225-800
Handled	60-90	100-225	225-800
SPOONER			
Upright	100-160	175-250	275 650
Footed	100-175	200-325	350-800
Tray	`90-150	175-250	250-550
SUGAR & CREAM			
Small	100-175	175-275	300-650
Medium	120-200	225-300	325-700
Large	200-275	300-475	500-1500
Footed	200-275	325-500	525-1500
Covered	175-25	275-475	500-1350
Lump Sugar	n/a	125-475	n/a
Sifter	n/a	250-475	n/a
SYRUP			
Small (all glass)	90-150	175-250	250-425
Small (silver top)	200-275	300-425	450-600
TRAYS			
Bread	`300-400	425-650	700-2400
Cake Low foot	375-625	650-775	800-2600
Cake Tall Footed	1800-2500	2500-5000	5000-8500
Two Piece			
Oval 10"-12"	500-800	850-1100	1200-3200
Oval 14"-18"	700-925	1000-1500	2200-4200
Rectangle 14"	600-800	900-1400	1500-4000
Round 12"-14"	600-800	850-1100	1200-3200
Handled 6"-8"	700-850	900-1200	1400-2800
Square 9"	450-850	900-1350	1400-2600
Acorn/Leaf	n/a	1400-1800	2000-4200
Shell	n/a	1500-2000	2000-5500
VASES			
Small 6"-8"	100-135	150-300	400-900
Medium 10"-14"	175-550	325-550	600-2000
Large 16"-20"	800-1300	1400-1800	2000-4200
Tubular 12"	175-300	350-600	800-2400
Urn	425-700	750-1050	1200-3800
Two Handled 12"	475-650	700-1100	1200-2600
Fan	400-475	500-750	800-1200
Hanging w/Chain	450-650	800-1200	1400-2800
Shower Five Piece	1600-1900	2000-2800	3000-3800
Epergne 25"-30"	4500-7500	7500-14000	15000-28000
Cornucopia	3200-3800	4000-5400	5500-7500